Heart speaks unto heart

Benedictus II xh

*Apostolic Journey
to the United Kingdom 2010*

September 16 - 19, 2010

ACKNOWLEDGEMENTS

My first great debt of gratitude is to the Fathers of the Oratory of St Philip Neri, Edgbaston, founded by Blessed John Henry Newman, in particular to the late Father Stephen Dessain, to Father Gregory Winterton, and to his successor as Provost and Actor, Father Paul Chavasse. Without the tireless work of these notable men over many years, the Cause of their Founder could not have progressed.

My profound thanks go also to His Eminence Keith Cardinal O'Brien, Archbishop of St Andrews and Edinburgh, President of the Bishops' Conference of Scotland, and to the Most Reverend Vincent Nichols, Archbishop of Westminster, President of the Bishops' Conference of England and Wales, and former Archbishop of Birmingham, for their Forewords and for their constant encouragement to me.

The Most Reverend Bernard Longley, Archbishop of Birmingham, also merits my sincere thanks for his Preface, and for the opportunity to serve the Catholic Church as his Press Secretary and as Press Secretary to the Archdiocese of Birmingham, roles in which I served Archbishop Nichols for nine years from October 2000.

I should like to thank all those who have contributed their reflections, so quickly and powerfully recapturing memorable moments from this historic Apostolic Journey of His Holiness, Pope Benedict XVI, to the United Kingdom.

I should like to thank Mark Wallace, Chairman of WRG Creative Communication Ltd, and in particular Lizzie Pocock, Production Assistant, for their personal help to me. WRG was the company employed by the Catholic Church to turn a Birmingham Park into a venue fit for the great purpose of staging the Beatification ceremony which they did so sensitively.

I should particularly like to thank Monsignor Peter Brignall, Vicar General of the Diocese of Wrexham, who administered what is now called the Sacrament of the Anointing of the Sick to me, as I lay unconscious in Bangor ITU following a massive sub-arachnoid brain haemorrhage on Thursday 17 August 1995. The doctors told my wife Stella that I had less than four hours to live and that if I survived I would have been in a vegetative state. God had other plans.

Another Catholic friend of mine, whose crucial help with this book I gratefully acknowledge, is Philip Bonn, an international consultant to charities and the representative of various Inter-Governmental Organisations and Non-Governmental Organisations accredited to the United Nations. Philip has assisted me as Associate Editor; and also hosted a splendid dinner in Whitehall in honour of Deacon Jack Sullivan and in celebration of the Papal Visit.

I would also like to thank my dear friend Kevin Grant, the best caption writer I have encountered, and whom I have known since the 1970s. He has been a tower of strength to me in many projects, not only in my writing about Church matters, but also in my writing about postage stamps and philately.

I should like to thank Abbot Cuthbert Johnson OSB, now chaplain at Saint Mary's Abbey, Oulton, Staffordshire, whom I have known since we first arrived at Saint Columba's College, the White Fathers' Junior Seminary situated near Melrose, on 11 September 1959, stalwart beside me in many enterprises; also Madeleine Beard the artist and writer and Maggie Doherty for their support and encouragement.

Special gratitude is due to Fergal Martin, General Secretary of the Catholic Truth Society and to his unflagging team: Stephen Campbell, Llima Cole, Piero Finaldi, Richard Brown and Glenda Swain for their imagination, patience and industry as we swept towards publication.

My gratitude goes also to my daughter Sarah for her support of Deacon Jack Sullivan and his wife Carol as Jack prepared to take his allotted place at the Beatification ceremony.

Thanks without measure go to my wife Stella without whose labours across the piece I could never have completed this work. Unflagging and unflappable, she has been my command and control, deftly drawing and holding people and things together, including myself on the harder days. Thanks also go to the Anglican Parish Church of St John the Baptist in Harborne where she works as Communications Secretary, for kindly allowing her extended leave to help me with this project; and also for their prayers.

BENEDICT XVI
AND BLESSED JOHN HENRY
NEWMAN

THE STATE VISIT 2010
THE OFFICIAL RECORD

EDITED BY PETER JENNINGS

ASSOCIATE EDITOR PHILIP BONN

CATHOLIC TRUTH SOCIETY
PUBLISHERS TO THE HOLY SEE

For Stella, Sarah and Joseph
with my love and prayers

The Publisher gratefully acknowledges permission to reproduce the many photographic and other images in this volume.

Pictures by **Peter Jennings**. Pages 7, 10, 16, 28 top, 30, 31 both, 32, 35, 36, 37, 38, 46, 47, 54 bottom left, 56 top, 57 bottom, 108 top, 118, 120 top, 135, 136 bottom, 155, 158 bottom, 159 top, 171, 174, 176 all, 177 top, 182, 183, 193, 194, 195 top, 206. Pictures by **Stella Jennings** at pages 12, 158 top, 159 bottom. Pictures courtesy of the **Fathers of the Birmingham Oratory** at pages 25, 34, 153, 167, 192, 202, 203. Picture courtesy of the Fathers of the Roman Oratory at page 24.

Special thanks go to **Marcin Mazur** and the Catholic Communications Network for photographs on the following pages: 11, 14, 53, 54, 56, 58, 59, 60, 61, 62, 63, 65, 75, 77, 79, 80, 81, 84, 85, 87, 89, 94, 95, 99, 100, 102, 108, 112, 113, 115, 117, 121, 122, 123, 124, 125, 126, 127, 128, 134, 136, 138, 139, 140, 141, 144, 146, 147, 148, 149, 150, 152, 157, 160, 165, 167, 168, 169, 172, 185, 190, 191, 199, 207 © Marcin Mazur/Catholic Church.

L'Osservatore Romano Photographic Service: 6, 8, 18, 41, 42, 43, 44, 49, 51, 52, 54, 55, 57, 64, 65, 74, 76, 78, 81, 82, 83, 86, 88, 89, 90, 91, 93, 98, 99, 101, 103, 104, 105, 106, 107, 110, 111, 112, 117, 119, 120, 124, 125, 129, 132, 133, 142, 143, 147, 151, 154, 156, 161, 162, 163, 166, 170, 172, 173, 175, 177, 178, 179, 180, 181, 184, 186, 187, 188, 189, 191, 195, 198, 199, 200, 201, 202 © L'Osservatore Romano Photographic Service.

PA Photos - Page 6: Peter Macdiarmid/PA Wire/Press Association Images. Page 9 LEFTERIS PITARAKIS/AP/Press Association Images. Page 19: Chris Radburn/PA Wire/Press Association Images. Page 50: DYLAN MARTINEZ/AP/Press Association Images. Page 59, 64: Andrew Milligan/PA Archive/Press Association Images. Page 73: PA Archive/Press Association Images. Page 92: Gregorio Borgia/AP/Press Association Images. Page 114: Lewis Whyld/AP/Press Association Images. Page 161: Matt Dunham/AP/Press Association Images. Page 164/5: Kirsty Wigglesworth/AP/Press Association Images. Page 168: David Jones/PA Wire/Press Association Images. Page 196: Martin Cleaver/AP/Press Association Images. **Cafod** - Page 17. **Corbis Images** - Page 21: © Erzbistum/epa/Corbis. Page 22: © epa/Corbis. Page 23: © Vatican Pool/Osservatore Romano/Immaginazione/Corbis. Page 70: © Douglas Kirkland/CORBIS. Page 72: © Historical Picture Archive/CORBIS. Page 109: © Bettmann/CORBIS. Page 175: © CLAUDIO ONORATI/epa/Corbis. **ISTOCKPHOTOS** - Page 39: © Jeremy Edwards/istockphotos. Page 130: © Andrew Barker/ istockphotos. Page 131: © Catherine Lane/istockphotos. **Getty Images** - Page 48: WPA Pool/Pool. **Paul McSherry** - Page 66: © Paul McSherry

Front cover: Blessed John Henry Newman by Sir John Everett Millais, 1881. Courtesy of the National Portrait Gallery, London. His Holiness Pope Benedict XVI and Her Majesty The Queen, pictured at the Palace of Hollyroodhouse, Edinburgh, on Thursday 16 September 2010 © L'Osservatore Romano.

Website: www.cts-online.org.uk

ISBN 978 1 86082 698 6

Contents

Pope Benedict XVI's State Visit to Britain was not only historic, but a tumultuous success.

This was not of course what many in the media predicted. The fact that they were proved to be so wrong was the result of several factors.

Firstly, Pope Benedict himself, as has happened elsewhere, charmed all who met him or saw him with his gentleness and courtesy. We should not overlook how much of the success of the visit was simply due to him. The Pope had a punishing schedule which he completed with aplomb and was coping in a language which is not his own. It was an extraordinary personal achievement.

Secondly, from the moment he landed in Edinburgh to the beatification of Cardinal Newman in Birmingham the British people - Catholic and non-Catholic alike - reacted with so much happiness to his presence among us. I will not easily forget the crowds along the road as his cavalcade on the first day raced from Edinburgh to Glasgow, nor the 200,000 people who thronged the streets of London as the Popemobile passed by on its way to Hyde Park and the Vigil there. Public enthusiasm buried metropolitan cynicism.

Thirdly, the pastoral events were themselves very moving. There was the majestic liturgy in both Westminster Abbey and Westminster Cathedral, and the inspiring broad social mix of the worshippers at the London Prayer Vigil and the open air masses in Glasgow and Cofton Park, Birmingham.

And then there was the message itself, conveyed most memorably in the Pope's address in Westminster Hall where he was received with enthusiasm as well as respect. In the very Hall which had witnessed the trial of the canonised Thomas More, Pope Benedict spoke about conscience and the relationship between faith and politics. The Pope argued that reason and the rule of law are not themselves sufficient to sustain our civilisation. We need ethical foundations for our policy making and political debate.

One of the great virtues of Pope Benedict's intelligent exposition of his arguments was that they brought forth extraordinarily interesting responses from some of his interlocutors, for example both the Chief Rabbi and the Archbishop of Canterbury. Altogether, Britain demonstrated again during the visit that it is a tolerant and moderate country where faith groups have a hugely important part to play.

These four days in September leave memories and echoes which will have lasting consequences down the years.

The Right Honourable the Lord Patten of Barnes CH PC
Chancellor of the University of Oxford
formerly Governor of Hong Kong

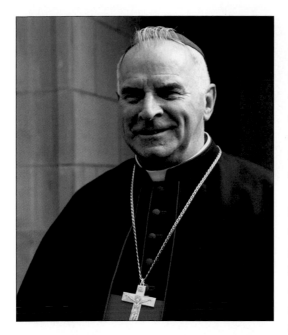

*I*t gives me very great pleasure to present this Foreword for the *Official Record of the State Visit to the United Kingdom by His Holiness Pope Benedict XVI.* As well as, of course, this being a State Visit, it was a wonderful opportunity for the Catholic Communities in Scotland and in England and Wales, as well as communities of other Christian denominations and other faiths and indeed those of no faiths at all – to show their love and appreciation for the apostolate of His Holiness Pope Benedict XVI.

It was indeed a special pleasure for the peoples of Scotland to have been able to thank Her Majesty The Queen, who received the Holy Father so graciously as soon as he arrived in Scotland at the beginning of the State Visit. We would also wish to put on record our deepest appreciation for the support of the Government of the United Kingdom, in particular the Foreign and Commonwealth Office, the Scottish Government, the City of Edinburgh Council and Glasgow City Council for their help and co-operation in the planning and delivery of a 'day of days' for over 200,000 people who saw the Holy Father during his time in our country. Many others had responsible positions to play in ensuring that everything 'went well' on the day itself and we would also wish to acknowledge the very positive coverage given to the Holy Father's time in our country by the broadcast and print media. Their expertise and commitment in relaying the Pope's message to the people of Scotland were greatly appreciated.

Arriving in Scotland, as he did, on Thursday 16 September 2010, the Feast of Saint Ninian, the Pope's words and his very presence among us reminded us of our ancient Christian heritage, as did that wonderful cavalcade of historical characters.

Preceded in the parade along Princes Street and led by 1,000 pipers, the Pope was greeted in a rapturous way by the 125,000 people – and showed that he was more than happy to be an honorary Scot for the day by wearing the 'Saint Ninian's Tartan' scarf, specially designed and woven for the Papal Visit.

The Mass at a crowded Bellahouston Park in Glasgow showed the joy of the pilgrims as they shared in this great prayer – while the periods of deep silence indicated their desire for union with God at this Mass, with ongoing prayerful and practical desire for collaboration with all the citizens in our country.

The joy of the Pope's visit to Scotland was continued in England and Wales where major events, both spiritual and temporal, allowed him to exchange with our Christian brothers and sisters, as well as our fellow Catholics, with civil society and with all people of goodwill. We were privileged to share in the joy of the Beatification of Cardinal John Henry Newman, having acknowledged his Scottish links with the Borders, where he came for relaxation and prayer.

Such a day and such days in the United Kingdom are deserving of a suitable recording for our own ongoing study and for those who will come after us. I am sure that the contents of this Official Record will provide such a source, both by way of the magnificent photographs and the accurate recording of the events of the day. May the spirit of this State Visit, accompanied by a pastoral visitation of his people by Pope Benedict XVI, long remain in our memories – while we thank our Holy Father himself, successor of Saint Peter, from the bottom of our hearts.

✠ His Eminence Keith Patrick, Cardinal O'Brien
Archbishop of St Andrews and Edinburgh
President of the Bishops' Conference of Scotland

+ Keith Patrick Cardinal O'Brien.

No one could have anticipated just how warmly Pope Benedict XVI was welcomed during his historic Apostolic Journey to the United Kingdom, handsomely recorded in this book. It was, of course, a State Visit, the first ever by a Pope. Yet beyond the solemnity of the occasion there was a warmth that was quite remarkable.

Everywhere he went, the Holy Father was met with excitement, joy and love. Of course there were some expressing disagreement, hostility and even, by a very few, hatred. But over 500,000 people came to express their respect and affection for the Pope.

Every moment of these historic days was available to a world-wide audience through the excellent media coverage given to the visit. The 'Big Assembly' on the second day was web-cast live into every Catholic school in our countries and by an interactive link to a school in Gambia. The visit was truly a global event.

For me the highlight of the visit was the astonishing reception given to the Holy Father by political and civic leaders in Westminster Hall. Never before had a Pope stood in that historic place, the cradle of democracy. The Pope's address there is worthy of careful study.

Every event in the visit had been carefully planned. Each was conducted with great dignity and often creating scenes of symmetry and deep beauty. Yet what will remain with me, as expressing some of the most powerful messages of the visit, are the periods of profound silence, filled with prayer, which marked the great outdoor liturgies. How can we ever forget the depth of the silence of 80,000 people in prayer before the Blessed Sacrament in Hyde Park? Such silence is golden and eloquent, beyond words, affirming that faith is not a problem but a great gift bringing peace and joy to our hearts.

I am sure that the joy of this visit permeated all its official moments, too. The Queen was radiant in extending her official welcome. The Prime Minister was generous in his invitation and most thoughtful in his remarkable speech of farewell. He described the Pope's visit as 'a great honour for our country' and assured the Holy Father that 'Faith is part of the fabric of our country. It always has been and it always will be.' Then he added: 'When you think of our country, think of it as one that not only cherishes faith, but one that is deeply, but quietly, compassionate.'

In this visit the Pope has given us so much. We thank him for the great personal effort he made, in every moment of each day, never stinting his generosity with individuals and with crowds.

Pope Benedict has given us a model of how we are to engage with our society when putting forward the things of faith. He has shown us the importance of open-heartedness, of genuine courtesy, of sensitivity to one's listeners, and of speaking clearly and reasonably especially on the difficult topics which have to be addressed.

The Holy Father has given us priorities in the witness we are to give: to the beauty of holiness, to the goodness and attractiveness of the truths of faith and to the joy and happiness that come from a relationship with Christ. Without these, the witness we want to give will not be effective.

Archbishop Vincent Nichols pictured on 3 April 2009, the day his appointment as Archbishop of Westminster was announced

He has also given us a clear focus in our proclamation of Christ. Christ is the one in whom we find forgiveness and healing. It is in his sacrifice on the Cross, made present for us in the Mass, that we learn again that there can be no love in our lives worthy of the name that does not include self-sacrifice. Christ leads us in this love and heals us so that we can start again.

This visit offered a wide embrace: to children and their teachers; to young people with their joy and high hopes; to leaders in and from other faiths and, of course, to our brothers and sisters in Christ, especially those so close to us in the Church of England.

At the climax of it all was the Beatification of Cardinal Newman. In a ceremony of stunning beauty, the Church in this country received a new model: of holiness, of pastoral care, of learned searching for the truth. This was a great and historic moment for it was an English Parish Priest who was declared Blessed and now has such a special place in our hearts.

I hope that all those who read this book will find, in doing so, that their memories of these days are refreshed. I hope that they will experience again the joy and happiness of this visit and sense again its invitation: 'Heart speaks unto heart!' The Lord is always seeking us and we thank Pope Benedict most warmly for making that so clear to us all.

✠ Vincent Nichols

✠ The Most Reverend Vincent Nichols
Archbishop of Westminster and
President of the Bishops' Conference of England and Wales

I am delighted to offer some words of introduction to this beautiful commemorative record of Pope Benedict XVI's Apostolic Journey and State Visit to the United Kingdom. I write this in the week immediately following the Holy Father's four days in Edinburgh and Glasgow, London and Birmingham when it seems that every conversation begins with people's personal memories of this remarkable and influential visit.

This was a time of extraordinary grace for the Catholic community in England and Wales and in Scotland. Pope Benedict, as our Supreme Pastor, set before us afresh the central themes of the Gospel, relating them to our own time and experience. In particular he strengthened our resolve to continue to play our part in public and civic life, confident that the significance of our faith can now be better understood by others who may not share it.

What we have witnessed and what this volume records was also a moment of great importance for all the people of our countries who welcomed Pope Benedict with a warmth that clearly moved him and in a way that confounded earlier critics of the visit. As he bade the Holy Father farewell, the Prime Minister voiced the view of many that Pope Benedict had made us sit up and listen. We have had an opportunity to see and hear the Holy Father as he truly is, and Pope Benedict in turn was able to see something of our national character at its best.

This Papal Visit has been as much to the people of the United Kingdom at-large as to the ten per cent who belong to the Catholic Church. It has also demonstrated the importance of a visit from the faith leader of nearly a fifth of the world's population to what is sometimes described as one of the most secularised societies in Europe. In so doing, the Holy Father has awakened the abiding, if impaired memory of the Christian roots that will always be the foundation of our society. He also leaves us with a challenge: how can we understand ourselves as a people and shape our future unless in relation to the God who is our only certain and unchanging point of reference?

The impact of Pope Benedict's visit has been felt not only by Christians, but by many others for whom faith in God is their compass-point in life. It highlights an opportunity and a challenge that Blessed John Henry Newman recognised in the changing society of his own time. It is not so much that the truth and beauty of God and the values offered by religion are being ignored or rejected, but our own attempts to express or share our faith sometimes fail to move our contemporaries. Pope Benedict's visit has encouraged Christians to search for new ways to touch the lives of others, and he has already begun the task for us.

For various reasons, people have been tempted to compare the Pastoral Visit made by Pope John Paul II in 1982 to this visit nearly thirty years later, in 2010. The world of 1982 was very different from today, and the freedom that people then enjoyed to attend all the papal gatherings has disappeared because of heightened security. Yet that didn't discourage large numbers from participating in the spiritual gatherings of Pope Benedict's visit or from flocking to greet him during his journeys in the Popemobile, as many of the photographs reproduced here will bear witness.

Another difference between the two Papal Visits arises from the contrasting characters of the two Pontiffs. Given his largeness of character, the persona of Pope John Paul II made an indelible impression on all who saw and heard him in 1982, and reinforced his message to the Catholic Church in the United Kingdom. Pope Benedict's gentle and courteous manner impressed in a different way as he reached out to engage with individuals and groups on this recent pilgrimage. His invitation to dialogue with the Catholic Church was modelled by the manner and mood of his many encounters, and the images of this volume surely capture that engaging quality.

I hope that this Official Record will bring to life many treasured memories of the Papal Visit for those who took part or who followed the excellent coverage on television, radio or internet. These

Archbishop Bernard Longley presents a copy of 'The Apologia' by Blessed John Henry Newman to the Holy Father

remarkable pictures bear witness to the number and variety of meetings that Pope Benedict included in his pilgrimage. They also remind us of the many unscheduled stops the Holy Father made in order to meet with and bless those who lined the streets of the cities he visited.

May the pages that follow draw you once again into the joy of being on pilgrimage with Pope Benedict, Servant of the Servants of God – may they vividly recall for you the four days that we shall never forget.

✠ The Most Reverend Bernard Longley
Archbishop of Birmingham

THE THIRD SPRING

The historic State Visit of our dear Holy Father, Pope Benedict XVI to the United Kingdom on the theme 'Heart Speaks unto Heart' in the year Two Thousand and Ten has heralded a Third Spring for the Catholic Church, for members of all Christian traditions and indeed for all people of faith in these islands. It is thus that a new and important phase has commenced in the long-standing relations between the Holy See and Great Britain.

Archbishop Bernard Longley with his Press Secretary Peter Jennings at Oscott College

In his Farewell Address to His Holiness Pope Benedict XVI, the Prime Minister, the Right Honourable David Cameron MP, said: 'Faith is part of the fabric of our country. It always has been and it always will be.' Mr Cameron concluded: 'I look forward to ever closer co-operation between the United Kingdom and the Holy See, as we redouble our resolve to work for the common good, both here in Britain and with our partners abroad.'

In recent times, the Catholic Church in the United Kingdom has faced many difficulties, some of them entirely self-inflicted. Against this, the inspirational and affirming words of the Holy Father spoken in Edinburgh, Glasgow, London and finally Birmingham have brought renewal, refreshment and, importantly, much-needed encouragement to millions of people.

As a fellow Birmingham resident (a Protestant originally from Northern Ireland) has observed to me, 'The Pope is a gracious, humble, sensitive and Godly man. He avoided nothing in his sermons and really challenged Britain to fight for its Christian heritage.'

God has blessed this land with a *kairos*, a special moment of grace. A remarkable sea-change has taken place in the relationship between the Catholic Church and the State. Ecumenical exchanges, in particular those between the Catholic Church and the Church of England, have consequently been rejuvenated and reinvigorated. Moreover, the relationships between the Catholic Church and other faiths in Great Britain, in particular Judaism and Islam, have also been strengthened. People of Faith in Britain now have a vital role to play, inspired by the Catholic Church, in striving for the Common Good in the multi-faith, multicultural society, of 21st-century Britain, a society which is at the same time both secular and consumerist.

Blessed John Henry Newman gave his famous sermon, The Second Spring, in the chapel of St Mary's College, Oscott, on 13 July 1852, to the assembled bishops, during the First Synod of Westminster. Pope Benedict XVI addressed the assembled bishops of England, Wales and Scotland, in the same chapel, one hundred and fifty-eight years later, on Sunday 19 September 2010.

The Holy Father told them: 'This has been a day of great joy for the Catholic community in these islands. Blessed John Henry Newman, as we may now call him, has been raised as an example of heroic faithfulness to the Gospel and as an intercessor for the Church in this land that he loved and served so well. Here in this very chapel in 1852, he gave voice to the new confidence and vitality of the Catholic community in England and Wales, after the restoration of the hierarchy, and his words could be applied equally to Scotland a quarter of a century later. His Beatification today is a reminder of the Holy Spirit's continuing action in calling forth gifts of holiness, from among the people of Great Britain, so that from east to west and from north to south, a perfect offering of praise and thanksgiving may be made to the glory of God's name.'

During his weekly General Audience in Saint Peter's Square on Wednesday 22 September 2010, Pope Benedict XVI said: 'I was bidden farewell by Prime Minister Cameron during a very cordial speech at Birmingham International Airport on the Government's wish to build a partnership for development with the Catholic Church and others.'

At the end of his address the Holy Father said: 'Sunday, then, was a moment of deep personal satisfaction, as the Church celebrated the blessedness of a great Englishman, whose life and writings I have admired for many years and who has come to be appreciated by countless people far beyond the shores of his native land. Blessed John Henry Newman's clear-minded search to know and express the truth in charity, at whatever cost to his own personal comfort, status and even friendship, is a wonderful testimony of a pure desire to know and love God in the communion of the Church. His, is surely an example that can inspire us all.'

Speaking for myself, I was privileged as a young boy to have been in the Blessed John Henry Newman Memorial Church, Edgbaston, when the Cause was first introduced in 1958, and to have worked on the Cause since the mid-1970s. I was also present in the organ gallery of the chapel at Oscott College at the meeting of the Holy Father with the Bishops of England and Wales, and Scotland, which took place shortly after the Beatification. I attended the High Mass in Thanksgiving for the Beatification of John Henry Newman at the Oratory in Birmingham, where the concelebrants included Fathers from the Oratories of Birmingham, London and Oxford, who were joined by representatives from many of the other Oratories throughout the world.

The Apostolic Journey of His Holiness, Pope Benedict XVI to the United Kingdom was given extensive and generally positive coverage by the media throughout the world, and the visit has been faithfully recorded in this book for the benefit of future generations. The forewords, preface and carefully selected post-visit reflections written by some of those who played an integral part in the visit, are intended to capture vividly and thoughtfully its special moments, which in themselves are already important parts of the history of Christianity in Great Britain.

There was a profound silence during the moving moments when more than 80,000 pilgrims adored the Blessed Sacrament in Hyde Park, during Evening Prayer on Saturday 18 September 2010. This took place on the eve of the Beatification of Cardinal Newman, the best-known English churchman of the 19th century. This silence was more eloquent than any introductory words of mine can be. God has richly blessed us with a special *kairos*. 'I do not ask to see the distant scene; one step enough for me.' (from *Lead, Kindly Light*, Blessed John Henry Newman).

Peter Jennings, Archdiocese of Birmingham
Feast of Our Lady of Walsingham
Friday 24 September 2010

THE UNITED KINGDOM AND THE HOLY SEE

The Prime Minister, the Right Honourable David Cameron MP, welcomes His Holiness Pope Benedict XVI to the United Kingdom

Tuesday 14 September 2010

Cardinal Newman was one of the greatest Englishmen, not just of his own times, but of any times. Like other courageous men and women of faith he believed passionately that we should follow our consciences. Many, too many, have died for that same cause. In Britain their numbers have included both Protestant and Catholic martyrs, like Thomas More, whose trial took place in Westminster Hall, where the Pope will address representatives of civil society from across our country.

At the end of his historic Visit to Britain this week, Pope Benedict XVI will beatify the Cardinal during Mass in a Birmingham park where the Cardinal used to take his recreation during his years as a simple parish priest in that great industrial city.

It will be a moving climax to the first Official Visit ever made to Britain by a pope.

I use the word historic for this visit. That can often be an over-worked cliché. But on this occasion it is wholly accurate. That is why television channels around the world will be covering every moment of the four days he spends with us.

As Britain's Prime Minister I welcome the fact that my predecessors first invited the Pope to visit this country and I am delighted that he accepted that invitation and the one he received from Her Majesty the Queen. He comes here as a Head of State and leader of a Church with over 6 million members in Britain and almost 1.2 billion around the world.

Like other faith groups, the Catholic Church proclaims a message of peace and justice to the world and we work closely with it in the furtherance of these causes.

Despite the tough times through which we are battling, we have ring-fenced spending on overseas development. The alleviation of poverty is one of the greatest challenges facing the world. The

grotesque condition in which too many live today, with disease and misery their constant companions, are a moral affront to all of us who live in comfort in rich countries.

The Catholic Church and its agencies are in the frontlines of the fight against poverty throughout the world. We work with them – organisations like CAFOD, SCIAF, Trócaire and Caritas – in Africa, Asia and Latin America. In sub-Saharan Africa, for example, Catholic agencies at local churches provide about a quarter of all primary education and healthcare, and an equally large part of the services for all those suffering from AIDS.

The Holy See is a partner in pursuit of the UN's Millennium Development Goals, which will be discussed at the United Nations Headquarters in New York again next week, at which the Deputy Prime Minister, Nick Clegg, will represent this country. For our part, we are totally committed to meeting the UN target of spending 0.7 per cent of our national income on aid by 2013. And we want to ensure that the money we spend goes to those who need it most. Sustainable economic development is closely linked to political stability and security. A world in which there is a yawning gap between the rich and the poor will be more dangerous and less secure for all of us.

We are also close partners of the global Catholic Church in the campaign against climate change. Once again, it is the poor who will suffer most if we do not act to moderate global warming. What is required is not just international agreement to abate carbon dioxide emissions, difficult as that is. We need to develop a new approach to economic growth, defining and pursuing it in ways that respect and preserve our natural environment.

The new British Government strongly believes in pushing decisions down to the local level, and in involving as many people and organisations as possible in working for and achieving the well-being of every community. The great 18th century Tory philosopher, Edmund Burke, called these parts of society, the 'little platoons' and argued that responsibility should be spread among them. I call it the 'Big Society' – where we're all in it together, where everyone pulls together and works together; a more responsible society, where we all

exercise our responsibilities to each other, to our families and to our communities. One where we don't just ask what are my entitlements, but what are my responsibilities.

Catholic social teaching has made a similar case for more than a century, and Catholic organisations work alongside other faith groups in education and welfare to make our country more harmonious and caring. Of course, the State has a role itself in promoting individual wellbeing, but this work should dovetail with what others do, not subvert it.

There has been a lot of exaggerated comment that Pope Benedict will this week be visiting a largely secular country. I do not agree with this and there is much evidence in polls and the attendance at religious services to contradict it. But in any case, I believe such comment misses the point. The Pope's visit should not just be welcomed by British Catholics or people of faith more broadly but by all who welcome what faith groups contribute to our society and who understand that for many faith is a gift to be cherished, not a problem to be overcome.

We may not always agree with the Holy See on every issue. But that should not prevent us from acknowledging that the Holy See's broader message can help challenge us to ask searching questions about our society and how we treat ourselves and each other.

Cardinal Newman once said that one little deed, whether by someone who helps 'to relieve the sick and needy' or someone who 'forgives an enemy'… evinces more true faith than could be shown by 'the most fluent religious conversation' or 'the most intimate knowledge of Scripture'.

Cardinal Newman is greatly remembered in Birmingham for his care for its people. During a cholera outbreak in the city, he worked tirelessly among the poor and sick. And when he himself died, the poor of the city turned out in their thousands to line the streets. Inscribed on the pall of his coffin was his motto, 'Heart speaks to heart'. Hardly surprisingly, it is the theme of this Papal Visit. I hope that it will be reflected in the warm welcome that Pope Benedict receives in Britain and in the sentiments that he leaves behind when he returns to Rome.

OUR MAN IN THE VATICAN

by His Excellency Mr Francis Campbell, Her Britannic Majesty's Ambassador to the Holy See (2005-2011)

*A*s the United Kingdom's Ambassador to the Holy See it has been my privilege since 2005 to help develop and strengthen an important relationship for Her Majesty's Government, and one which in 2010 reaches a new milestone: the first Official Visit by the Pope to the United Kingdom. The United Kingdom's relationship with the Holy See touches on a wide range of global issues where we have many shared interests and objectives, and the State Visit of His Holiness Pope Benedict XVI will be an unprecedented opportunity both to celebrate what has been achieved so far in these areas, and to look ahead at how we might jointly address future challenges.

The Catholic Church plays a unique role on the world stage. It is active at both the global and local level, whether through delivering healthcare and education at the grassroots level, or lobbying world leaders on important global issues such as conflict resolution, disarmament and climate change. The Catholic Church's global presence gives it a unique position in the fight against poverty in the most vulnerable parts of the world.

The Holy See is the universal government of the Catholic Church and operates from the Vatican City State, a sovereign, independent territory of 0.17 square miles. The Holy See acts and speaks for the whole Catholic Church. Recognised in international law as a sovereign juridical entity, headed by the Pope, the Holy See maintains diplomatic relations with 178 states, and is recognised as a permanent observer state at the United Nations.

The Holy See is therefore a sovereign entity with an unusually large global reach. The Catholic Church is a global institution with over 1.15 billion adherents (17.5 per cent of the world's population, including some 10 per cent of the United Kingdom population); reaching into every corner of the planet through its 500,000 priests, 800,000 sisters and nuns, and 219,655 parishes; serious influence in as many countries as are in the Commonwealth; a privileged status as interlocutor with the two other Abrahamic faiths – Islam and Judaism – and two generations of experience in inter-faith dialogue and many centuries of co-existence. The Holy See is one of the world's oldest organisations, with a continuous history from the period of Emperor Constantine in the 4th century AD.

*T*he Crown's first resident ambassador, John Shirwood, was sent by King Edward IV to the Pope in 1479, hence the Embassy to the Holy See is the United Kingdom's oldest. Formal diplomatic relations between the Crown and the Holy See were interrupted in 1536. Links were restored in 1553, but ceased again in 1559 until they were restored formally in 1914. However, unofficial ties between the United Kingdom and the Holy See were maintained through much of the 18th and 19th centuries. The United Kingdom re-established resident diplomatic relations with the Holy See in 1914. These were raised to full Ambassadorial status in 1982, coinciding with the pastoral visit of Pope John Paul II to the United Kingdom in that year.

Since his election in April 2005, Pope Benedict XVI has frequently spoken out on international themes and issues, such as the need to protect the environment and tackle climate change, address the plight of the poor in developing countries, and find ways to resolve conflicts around the world. So the Holy See is often at the cutting edge of policy-making on many global issues, and it is here that the United Kingdom's relationship with the Holy See has its principal focus.

International Development

The Holy See is a crucial partner to the international community if we are to deliver on the Millennium Development Goals by 2015. In view of this, Pope Benedict XVI has written regularly to world leaders ahead of G8 and G20 Summits, reminding governments not to forget the plight of the poor in the developing world. Overall, aid increases and debt cancellation have helped to get 40 million more children into school. The number of people with access to AIDS treatment has increased from just 100,000 to over four million. The proportion of the world's population living in poverty has fallen from a third to a quarter.

The Holy See's contribution is key to that continuing success. The Catholic Church alone is reckoned to be the world's second largest international development body after the United Nations (UN). Caritas Internationalis, the social arm of the Catholic Church, is a Vatican body which brings together some 160 national Catholic aid agencies under a single umbrella - including the Catholic Fund for Overseas Development (CAFOD) in England & Wales, and the Scottish International Aid Fund (SCIAF) in Scotland. More than 50 per cent of the hospitals in Africa are operated under the auspices of faith-based organisations, with the Catholic Church in Africa being responsible for nearly one-quarter of all healthcare provision. The Catholic Church is one of the biggest global health providers. It runs 5,246 hospitals, 17,530 dispensaries, 577 leprosy clinics, and 15,208 houses for the elderly, chronically ill and people with physical and learning disabilities worldwide. Its agencies provide a quarter of all HIV/AIDS care in Africa. In education too, the Catholic Church provides around 12 million school places in Sub-Saharan Africa, thereby offering educational opportunities to enable millions of young people to get out of poverty.

The United Kingdom warmly welcomes the work of Catholic organisations in many of the poorest countries of the world, including in the Commonwealth, and our Embassies maintain a dialogue with local Catholic organisations aimed at finding ways to bring about positive outcomes. An example of the United Kingdom's close collaboration with the Holy See in recent years has been on developing new ways to finance

international development. The International Finance Facility (IFF) uses financial markets to front-load development spending. Launched at the Vatican in 2004, Pope John Paul II gave the concept his full moral support.

In November 2006, Pope Benedict XVI went a step further and purchased the first Immunisation Bond (IFFIm). This Bond has raised over $1.6 billion for immunisation programmes in 70 of the world's poorest countries. These funds will prevent five million child deaths by 2015, as well as more than five million future adult deaths, by protecting more than 500 million children against measles, tetanus, and yellow fever. The United Kingdom's joint work with the Holy See on the Immunisation Bond, and the Pope's participation from the very outset, helped spread the global message about the Bond and make it a success. Meanwhile, the United Kingdom Government has renewed its own pledge to commit 0.7 per cent of Gross National Income to international development by 2013.

The Environment

The Holy See has been at the forefront of international efforts to protect the environment and tackle climate change. Pope Benedict's 2009 Encyclical *Caritas in Veritate* focused strongly on environmental issues, calling on the international community to counter mistreatment of the environment, to work to ensure that the costs of exploiting resources are borne by those who incur them, not by future generations; and stressing that the protection of the environment and the climate requires full international co-operation, including with the weakest regions of the world.

The Holy See has also led on practical steps. The Vatican City State is on track to becoming the world's first carbon neutral state, offsetting its emissions through the planting of trees and installing solar panels. It also recently announced plans to build Europe's largest solar farm on 740 hectares to the north of Rome, which will produce enough energy to power over 40,000 homes and exceed the European Union's renewable energy targets of 20 per cent of demand by 2020. The United Kingdom is working with the Holy See

to raise awareness of the consequences of climate change around the world, for example through our South America Climate Change Network. This year the Government of the United Kingdom has given its full support to the 10:10 campaign aimed at reducing carbon emissions by 10 per cent in 2010.

But as important as those practical steps are, the real influence of the Holy See rests in its moral weight. While some will be persuaded to address climate change by self-interest as a result of the economic or scientific evidence, the Holy See is well-placed to articulate the moral argument that will shift the momentum toward political and social action.

The British Ambassador to the Holy See was among the first to welcome the Holy Father to Scotland

Disarmament

On the disarmament agenda, the United Kingdom and the Holy See have a number of shared objectives. The Holy See played an important role in achieving the international consensus required to agree a Convention on Cluster Munitions in 2008. It was among the first states to sign the new treaty, and this leadership helped build the momentum which led to the Convention coming into effect on 1 August 2010. Similarly, in 2009 the Holy See played an important role in encouraging 153 states to support a United Nations General Assembly Resolution on moving ahead with an Arms Trade Treaty. That crucial vote brought us a step closer to what Pope Benedict called for in 2008, when he exhorted 'all persons involved in the sale or traffic of arms, with interests that are often extremely lucrative, to ask themselves what are the consequences engendered by their behaviour. [...] May the international community commit itself in this field together with the local authorities so that peace in all countries will gain ground every day.' With over 2.1 million people having died from armed violence in the last three years, the Holy See has been a strong supporter of the Arms Trade Treaty since the outset.

It is clear that the Holy See is in a unique position to help the international community meet a range of global challenges, such as eradicating poverty, encouraging disarmament, and combating climate change. On these and other issues the United Kingdom and the Holy See share a common vision, hence the relationship that has built up between us is an important and productive one. As we welcome Pope Benedict XVI on his momentous visit to the United Kingdom, we also look forward to developing our understanding and co-operation still further in the period ahead.

His Excellency Mr Francis Campbell, Her Britannic Majesty's Ambassador to the Holy See, 2005 - 2011, after which he will take up his appointment as Deputy High Commissioner to India, based in Karachi.

THE STATE DINNER

*T*he following joint communiqué was released: Her Majesty's Government hosted a dinner at Lancaster House, London, on Friday 17 September 2010 for the Holy See delegation accompanying Pope Benedict XVI on his Official Visit to the United Kingdom, headed by Cardinal Secretary of State, Tarcisio Bertone.

The United Kingdom side was headed by the Right Honourable William Hague, the Foreign Secretary. Those present included a number of senior British government ministers and senior officials from the Holy See. The discussion covered a range of areas of shared interest between the United Kingdom government and the Holy See.

Her Majesty's Government and the Holy See share a commitment to bringing an end to poverty and underdevelopment. On the eve of a summit in New York to review progress towards implementing the Millennium Development Goals, they share the conviction that more needs to be done to address the unnecessary suffering caused by hunger, diseases and illiteracy. Strong political leadership and respect for the ethos of local communities are necessary in the promotion of the right to life, food, health and development for all.

The Foreign Secretary, William Hague, welcomes the Vatican Secretary of State, Cardinal Tarcisio Bertone

The British Government and the Holy See share a conviction of the urgent need for action to address the challenge of climate change. Action is needed at every level from the governmental to the individual if we are to rapidly reduce greenhouse gas emissions, to set in motion the transition to a global low-carbon economy, and to assist poor and vulnerable countries to adapt to the impacts of climate change that are already inevitable.

We had a good exchange of views on a variety of social and economic issues, recognising the essential role played by faith in the lives of individuals and as part of the fabric of a strong, generous, and tolerant society.

HIS HOLINESS POPE BENEDICT XVI

Pope Benedict XVI - 'A Simple Labourer in the Vineyard of the Lord'

by Abbot Cuthbert Johnson OSB

The small Bavarian village of Marktl am Inn lies between Munich and Passau, a somewhat typical and picturesque small town, but of little interest to the tourist and little more than a name on a road sign to the traveller. All of this changed dramatically when one of its sons appeared on the central loggia of St Peter's Basilica on Tuesday 19 April 2005 as Pope Benedict XVI.

The Holy Father greets Abbot Cuthbert Johnson

The villagers were proud of their Cardinal and a plaque marked the house where he was born, but the news that Joseph Alois Ratzinger had been elected as the Successor to Pope John Paul II and the 264th successor of Saint Peter filled the town with immense joy. The parish church bells rang out, and a traditional Bavarian gun salute was fired, before the people assembled in church for a Mass of thanksgiving. In the evening the village celebrated with music, and Bavarian beer was served freely to all who had come to congratulate the town on the singular honour that had been conferred upon it.

Joseph Alois Ratzinger was born at number 11 Schulstrasse, Marktl, on 16 April 1927 which happened to be Holy Saturday and so fittingly, he was baptised the same day. His father, whose name was also Joseph, was a police officer who served the Bavarian Ordnungspolizei until his retirement in 1937, when the family moved to the town of Traunstein, a small village near the Austrian border, about twenty miles from Salzburg. His mother, Maria Peintner, came from Bolzano-Bozen in the South Tyrol, which is now part of Italy.

Joseph Alois was the youngest of three children. His brother Georg, born in 1924, showed talent as a musician at an early age, and he was eventually to become Director of the illustrious Regensburg Cathedral Choir, originally founded in 975. Along with his younger brother, Georg was also ordained

to the priesthood in 1951. Their sister Maria, who never married, was her brother Joseph's housekeeper until her death in Rome in 1991.

The Ratzinger family, like many other devout German Catholic families, were troubled by the rise of the Nazi regime and its hostility towards the Catholic Church. Joseph and Maria Ratzinger needed to be firm in the upbringing of their children in that difficult historical period. They gave them a deep grounding and knowledge of their faith which was to sustain all three children in the period leading up to, and during, the dark years of the Second World War.

With the return of peace to Europe the work of rebuilding began. Not only were buildings in need of reconstruction but also society itself. The Church too had suffered from the devastation of war and persecution, and Joseph and his brother Georg began training for the priesthood at the seminary in Freising, going on to study at the Ludwig-Maximilian University in Munich.

On the Feast of the Apostles Peter and Paul, June 29 1951, the Ratzinger brothers, Joseph and Georg, were ordained to the priesthood in Freising by Cardinal Michael von Faulhaber, Archbishop of Munich.

The young priest, Joseph Ratzinger, was destined for further studies. His attraction towards the teaching of Saint Augustine led to his presentation in 1953 of a dissertation entitled '*The People and the*

Archive photograph of the now Pope Benedict (standing right) pictured with his family

House of God in Augustine's Doctrine of the Church'. A further research dissertation on the '*The Theology of History in Saint Bonaventure*', presented in 1957, qualified him for professorial work.

Professor Joseph Ratzinger took up his first important post at the University of Bonn in 1959 with an inaugural lecture entitled 'The God of Faith and the God of Philosophy'. His reputation as a theologian grew and he was offered a place at the University of Münster which he accepted in 1963.

This was a period of great ferment in the Church. Pope, now Blessed, John XXIII, had called an Ecumenical Council which opened in 1962. The Archbishop of Cologne, Cardinal Joseph Frings, appointed Professor Ratzinger as his theological advisor. As an accredited 'Expert', Joseph Ratzinger was able to follow the work of the Council at close quarters even though he did not formally participate in its work.

Speaking of this important period in his life, Pope Benedict declared: 'I had the wonderful opportunity to be present at the Second Vatican Council as an expert; this was a very great time of my life, in which I was able to be part of this meeting, not only between bishops and theologians, but also between continents, different cultures, and different schools of thinking and spirituality in the Church'.

Given his historical and philosophical formation and background, Professor Ratzinger accepted in 1966 a chair in Dogmatic Theology at the University of Tübingen, because of the historical and ecumenical approach to the study of theology that was prevalent in that University.

His years at Tübingen were academically enriching and helped develop a certain breadth of vision in the Professor's theological thought and reflection. This fruitful development was interrupted in 1968, not only by the general student unrest of that year but also by what he described as 'a very violent explosion of Marxist theology'. His unhappiness with the change of circumstances at Tübingen led him to accept without hesitation the offer of a position at the then newly founded University of Regensburg.

Professor Ratzinger wanted to play a role in developing a new University and at the same time develop his theological work in peaceful surroundings. In fact, during his period at Regensburg he wrote some of his important theological works. He held the Chair of Dogmatics and the History of Dogma and was also Vice-President of the University. In 1972, together

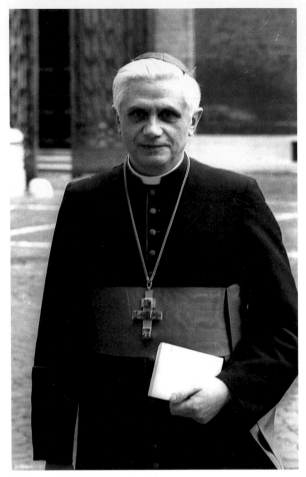

His Eminence Joseph Cardinal Ratzinger

with Henri de Lubac, Hans Urs von Balthasar and other well-known theologians, he founded the journal '*Communio*' which has made an important contribution to the development of Catholic theological thought.

The years spent at Regensburg were both fruitful and enriching, and from the human point of view he also had the pleasure of being close to his brother who was then Choirmaster of the Cathedral. This period of his life was brought to a close in 1977 when Pope Paul VI named him Archbishop of Munich and Freising.

As Cardinal Archbishop of Munich, the formal academic aspect of his ministry came to an end, but it formed the foundation for his pastoral ministry and preaching of the Word of God. When explaining the choice of his episcopal motto 'Co-operators of the truth' he underlined the continuity of his priestly ministry: 'On the one hand I saw it as the relation between my previous task as professor and my new mission. In spite of different approaches, what was involved, and continued to be so, was following the truth and being at its service. On the other hand I chose that motto because in today's world the theme of truth is omitted almost entirely, as something too great for man, and yet everything collapses if truth is missing.'

His academic foundation and his pastoral experience were to be united in 1981 when Pope John Paul II appointed Cardinal Joseph Ratzinger, Prefect of the Congregation for the Doctrine of the Faith. This position also included the Offices of President of the Pontifical Biblical Commission and of the International Theological Commission.

During nearly twenty-five years as Prefect of the Congregation for the Doctrine of the Faith, Cardinal Ratzinger proved to be a most loyal 'Co-operator of the truth' in his service of the Church and the Holy Father, Pope John Paul II.

In the media he was often portrayed as a severe enforcer of Church Law and Discipline. Clarity of thought and prudent action were the true marks of his ministry as Prefect. Many who visited him, even in difficult circumstances, were always impressed by his gentleness and understanding, recognising that he always sought 'to speak the truth in charity'. Cardinal Ratzinger was not simply courteous and kind; these human qualities were rooted in his exercise of the virtue of humility.

Cardinal Ratzinger had been appointed Dean of the Sacred College of Cardinals in 2002 and so it fell to him three years later to preside over the funeral of Pope John Paul II on 8 April 2005 - six days after his death on 2 April - and also over the Mass which opened the Conclave for the Pontifical election (and which elected him Pope).

Despite his 78 years, Cardinal Ratzinger was still evidently in good health and clearly made a very favourable impression on his fellow members of the College of Cardinals. Consequently, after only four ballots, the 115 Cardinal Electors from 52 countries across five continents elected him Bishop of Rome and Successor of Peter.

During his first public Audience held in St Peter's Square, 27 April 2005, the Pope said: 'I wish to speak of why I chose the name Benedict. Firstly, I remember Pope Benedict XV, that courageous prophet of peace, who guided the Church through turbulent times of war. In his footsteps, I place my ministry in the service of reconciliation and harmony between peoples. Additionally I recall Saint Benedict of Nursia, co-patron of Europe, whose life evokes the Christian roots of Europe. I ask him to help us all to hold firm to the centrality of Christ in our Christian life: May Christ always take first place in our thoughts and action.'

Someone who was present at the early Audiences in St Peter's Square made an interesting observation: 'The pilgrims', he said, 'used to come to see Pope John Paul II. Now they come to listen to Pope Benedict XVI.'

Continuity is a key word in reflecting upon the life and work of Joseph Alois Ratzinger, Pope Benedict XVI. Just as he saw no break in his own personal development when he left the academic world to take upon himself the pastoral responsibility of the archdiocese of Munich; and just as he integrated his academic and pastoral experience when he undertook the task of Prefect of the Congregation for the Doctrine of the Faith; so too, his Pontificate is marked by the desire for that continuity which is founded in the love of the living tradition of the Church. Joseph Ratzinger has never lost sight of the vision of the Second Vatican Council and as Pope Benedict XVI seeks faithfully to implement it with sincerity and clarity.

The subjects of his Encyclical Letters also provide a key to understanding his mind. Pope Benedict XVI, following Saint Paul's example, seeks to be rooted in Charity, unwavering in Hope and firm in the Faith.

Shortly after his election, during his appearance on the balcony of St Peter's Basilica, in his greeting to the faithful, Pope Benedict XVI declared himself to be: 'A simple, humble labourer in the vineyard of the Lord'.

Away from his desk, altar and audience Pope Benedict relaxes at his piano

In such a role Pope Benedict has placed himself in the past, and such he will aspire to remain, preferring in the words of his patron, Saint Benedict: 'To put the love of Christ before all else' and in all his undertakings seeking to ensure 'that in all things God may be glorified.'

I had the wonderful opportunity to be present at the Second Vatican Council as an expert; this was a very great time of my life.

- Pope Benedict XVI

CARDINAL NEWMAN (1801-1890)

A brief biography of Blessed John Henry Newman read by Father Richard Duffield, Provost of the Birmingham Oratory and Actor of the Newman Cause, during the Mass of Beatification

Cofton Park, Birmingham
Sunday 19 September 2010

John Henry Newman was born in London in 1801. He was for over twenty years an Anglican clergyman and a Fellow of Oriel College, Oxford. As a preacher, theologian and leader of the Oxford Movement, he was a prominent figure in the Church of England. His studies of the early Church drew him progressively towards full communion with the Catholic Church. With his companions he withdrew to a life of study and prayer at Littlemore, outside Oxford, where in 1845 Blessed Dominic Barberi, a Passionist priest, received him into the Catholic Church.

In 1847 he was himself ordained priest in Rome and, encouraged by Blessed Pope Pius IX, he went on to found the Oratory of St Philip Neri in England. He was a prolific and influential writer on a variety of subjects, including the development of Christian doctrine, faith and reason, the true nature of conscience, and university education. In 1879 he was created Cardinal by Pope Leo XIII. Praised for his humility, his life of prayer, his unstinting care of souls and contributions to

St Philip Neri, *by Guido Reni (1575-1642), Santa Maria in Vallicella (Chiesa Nuova), Rome*

the intellectual life of the Church, he died in the Birmingham Oratory which he had founded on 11 August 1890.

Cardinal Newman is mainly, on the one hand, a modern man, who took on all of the problems of modernity, he experienced the problem of agnosticism, the impossibility of knowing God, of believing; a man who throughout his life was on a journey, a journey to let himself be transformed by the truth, in a search of great sincerity and great willingness, to learn more, to find and to accept the path to true life.

- Pope Benedict XVI

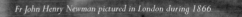

Fr John Henry Newman pictured in London during 1866

SPECIAL POSTAGE STAMPS TO COMMEMORATE THE STATE VISIT

A 'stamp of approval' for the State Visit of His Holiness Pope Benedict XVI and the Beatification of Cardinal Newman

by Peter Jennings

Two postage stamps depicting photographs of Cardinal Newman, one never published before, and a stamp label showing Pope Benedict XVI, were included in a souvenir miniature sheet issued by the Isle of Man Post Office on 11 August 2010. The date was the 120th Anniversary of the death of Cardinal Newman.

The two stamps, valued at £1.50 each, received Royal Approval from Her Majesty The Queen and included the Royal Cipher.

This remarkable sheet was released to commemorate the State Visit of His Holiness Pope Benedict XVI to the United Kingdom, 16-19 September 2010 and the Beatification of Cardinal Newman at Cofton Park, Birmingham, on Sunday 19 September.

The left-hand stamp depicts a previously unknown original photograph of Cardinal Newman taken by H J Whitlock, Photographers of New Street, Birmingham, and signed by Cardinal Newman, aged 82, at the Oratory House on Passion Sunday, 11 March 1883, for a visitor. The photograph was given to this correspondent by Father Charles Stephen Dessain (1907-1976), whose family were personal friends of Cardinal Newman and who had joined the community at the Oratory of St Philip Neri in Edgbaston, in 1929. Father Dessain, a distinguished scholar in Newman studies, and archivist from 1955, masterminded and edited the first 15 volumes of *The Letters and Diaries of John Henry Newman*, published in 32 volumes.

The right-hand stamp shows an original photograph of Dr Newman taken c. 1866 by McLean & Haes, Photographers, Haymarket, London.

The picture of Pope Benedict XVI by this author on the stamp label was taken during a General Audience in St Peter's Square, Rome, on Wednesday 10 June 2009.

The focal point of the sheet is an illustration of Cardinal Newman lying in state in the Oratory Church, Edgbaston before his Funeral Mass on Tuesday 19 August 1890, taken from *The Illustrated London News* of the time.

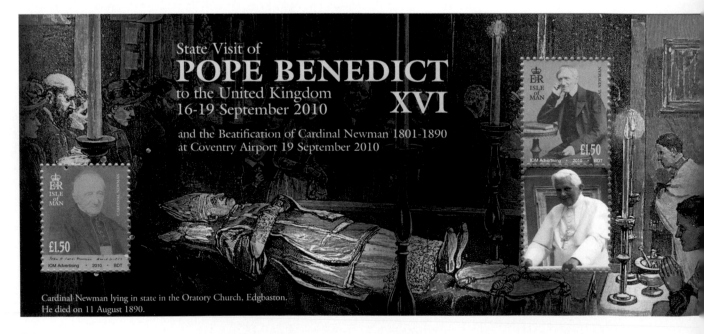

State Visit of **POPE BENEDICT XVI** to the United Kingdom 16-19 September 2010 and the Beatification of Cardinal Newman 1801-1890 at Coventry Airport 19 September 2010

Cardinal Newman lying in state in the Oratory Church, Edgbaston. He died on 11 August 1890.

John H /ard. Newman March 11.1883
H. J. WHITLOCK, PHOTO.   BIRMINGHAM

The front of the presentation pack shows: A drawing of Cardinal Newman at the Oratory House, Rednall (old spelling) on the outskirts of Birmingham, dated 22 July 1881; The Pectoral Cross belonging to Cardinal Newman recovered from his grave in the community graveyard at the Oratory House, Rednal, on 2 October 2008; The first verse of his famous hymn *Lead, Kindly Light*, in Newman's handwriting. The poem was written by John Henry Newman on 16 June 1833 while he was aboard a ship in the Mediterranean travelling from Palermo to Marseilles.

John Henry Newman was the greatest English religious figure of the 19th century. Today he is known world-wide as one of the foremost theologians of the Catholic Church and a prolific writer - he left more than 20,000 letters - but most of all he is revered as a much-loved holy parish priest in Birmingham. Cardinal Newman died in his room at the Oratory House, Edgbaston, aged 89, on Monday 11 August 1890.

The miniature sheet, a presentation pack, a first-day cover and an informative insert with background information were printed by BDT in Ireland by offset lithography process on PVA gummed paper during the early months of 2010. Supplies were sent to agencies and distributors before the announcement on 24 June 2010 that the Holy See had requested a change of venue for the Beatification of Cardinal Newman from Coventry Airport to Cofton Park in Birmingham, situated close to the Oratory Retreat at Rednal where Cardinal Newman was buried in the community graveyard.

The miniature sheet and the philatelic products wrongly refer to the Beatification of Cardinal Newman taking place: 'at Coventry Airport, 19 September 2010.'

These special stamps depicting Cardinal Newman will be collected and treasured by stamp collectors and non-collectors alike throughout the world. The inclusion of the Coventry Airport venue added considerable philatelic interest and captured the attention of the media.

The commemorative stamps and related products were the idea of this correspondent, a Fellow of the Royal Philatelic Society of London, who wrote the text and supplied the pictures to Isle of Man Stamps and Coins and worked by telephone and email with designer Stacey Smith, at Isle of Man Advertising & PR Ltd.

The miniature sheet was launched by the Most Reverend Bernard Longley, Archbishop of Birmingham, at the end of a press conference about the Papal Visit to the Archdiocese of Birmingham, held at Cathedral House, Birmingham, on 23 July 2010.

Archbishop Longley said: 'Once again postage stamps show their remarkable ability to inform and raise people's awareness of historic celebrations or important national and local events.

'Isle of Man Stamps and Coins are to be congratulated on these engaging and imaginative stamps, included in a special miniature sheet to commemorate the State Visit of Pope Benedict XVI and the Beatification of Cardinal John Henry Newman. This is first time that a Pope has been welcomed to the United Kingdom on a State Visit and these stamps highlight the importance of such a visit for the United Kingdom and Isle of Man citizens within and beyond the Catholic Church.'

The Archbishop of Birmingham added: 'The Beatification of Cardinal Newman promotes this man of God as an example of holiness and as the bearer of truth. He is a figure of international significance and these Isle of Man stamps will introduce Cardinal Newman and his witness to goodness and truth, to many people throughout the world who may not yet know him.'

The back of the first-day cover includes a specially written 'Welcome to His Holiness Pope Benedict XVI' by His Eminence Cardinal Keith O'Brien, Archbishop of St Andrews and Edinburgh, President of the Bishops' Conference of Scotland; and The Most Reverend Vincent

Archbishop Bernard Longley gives his stamp of approval

Nichols, Archbishop of Westminster, President of the Bishops' Conference of England and Wales.

The Isle of Man Post Office and the Holy See Post Office have issued a prestigious souvenir cover with special hand stamp cancellations to mark the Beatification of Cardinal Newman by Pope Benedict XVI at Cofton Park, Birmingham, on Sunday 19 September 2010. The Isle of Man hand stamp is in gold foil. Cofton Park is situated close to the Oratory Retreat, Rednal, where Cardinal Newman was buried in the community grave yard following his death at the Oratory House, Edgbaston, about eight miles away.

Because the original miniature sheet included the name of the wrong venue it was unsuitable for use on the joint Isle of Man and Holy See cover. Isle of Man Stamps and Coins and this author hit upon an ingenious solution. This involved cutting the original printed sheet and using only the right-hand third of the sheet, a single £1.50 stamp depicting Cardinal Newman and the stamp label showing Pope Benedict XVI.

The Most Reverend Vincent Nichols, Archbishop of Westminster, gave his stamp of approval to the original miniature sheet. He said: 'I am pleased to welcome the joint initiative of the Holy See and the Isle of Man in issuing a special cover for the postage stamp marking the State Visit of Pope Benedict XVI to the United Kingdom and the Beatification of Cardinal John Henry Newman.' The former Archbishop of Birmingham added: 'These historical events are fittingly recorded by this memorable cover with its additional hand stamp.'

The Vatican Information Service announced on 14 September 2010: 'The Vatican Post Office has issued a new postmark for the visit of Pope Benedict XVI to the United Kingdom.

It shows the figures of the Holy Father and of the new blessed accompanied by the words: 'BEATIFICATION OF CARDINAL NEWMAN'.

The presentation pack also includes illustrations of the first two stamps to depict Cardinal Newman. The Republic of Ireland issued a 2d and 1s. 3d value stamps on 19 July 1954, to commemorate the Centenary of the Founding of the Catholic University of Ireland by Dr Newman, the first Rector.

The island of Jersey included the portrait of Cardinal Newman by W. W. Ouless, RA, 1848-1933 on the 8p value in a set of four stamps issued on 20 September 1983 to mark the 50th Anniversary of the death of the artist. It was this portrait of the new Blessed John Henry Newman that was unveiled electronically during the Mass of Beatification at Cofton Park, Birmingham. The original painting is in the Oratory House, Edgbaston.

Special commemorative cover released jointly by the Isle of Man and the Holy See

THE HISTORY OF THE NEWMAN CAUSE

A unique insight into the history of the Newman Cause

by the Reverend Father Gregory Winterton

The Beatification of Cardinal John Henry Newman, by the Holy Father, Pope Benedict XVI, at Cofton Park in Birmingham on Sunday 19 September 2010 is a significant step in the history of Newman's Cause but is not the end of the story. Efforts will continue unabated to get the Cardinal canonised and, please God, made a Doctor of the Church, in order to give universal authority to Newman's teaching and the example of his life.

In order for this to happen the Church requires a second miracle, usually of physical healing, brought about through the intercession of Cardinal Newman.

So the message of all those connected with advancing his cause is simple, 'Please keep on praying' and if you have sick friends and relatives ask Blessed John Henry Cardinal Newman to intercede for them. Blessed John Henry Newman prayer cards for this purpose are available from the Catholic Truth Society.

To get the Newman Cause this far has taken a considerable time. Cardinal Newman died on 11 August 1890 but it was not until 1958 that his Cause was officially introduced. Two reasons especially held things up. Firstly, Cardinal Newman left behind a vast number of letters - nearly 20,000 - diaries, sermons, published and unpublished, memoranda and many other papers, and these needed to be sorted and catalogued by busy priests engaged in pastoral work. This took a significant amount of time, which was added to by the delay caused by the First World War, 1914-1918. Secondly, as Oratory Fathers 'love to be unknown', a number of the older fathers, some of whom were members of the community with Cardinal Newman, were not in favour of advancing his Cause.

During the Second World War, however, two foreign influences began to advance things - a book on Newman's Holiness by Father Louis Bouyer of the French Oratory, later translated into English; and an article in the journal *America* in the USA, suggesting that Newman's Cause should be advanced.

This last idea was taken up by Monsignor Dr H. Francis Davis, Vice Rector of St Mary's College, Oscott, the Archdiocese of Birmingham's Seminary, who approached English-speaking Bishops worldwide. Their whole-hearted support resulted in the Fathers of the Birmingham Oratory agreeing to the introduction of the Cause, which was solemnly done by Archbishop Francis Grimshaw on 17 June 1958 at the Newman Memorial Church, Edgbaston (known as the Birmingham Oratory).

At the time, English Catholics were not very well acquainted with how to go about promoting the Causes of Saints. In this case, they first thought of trying the process by the 'ordinary' method of calling witnesses to Newman's sanctity. But by 1958 only a few witnesses to the end of Newman's life were alive, including our own Father Denis Sheil who was the last Oratorian novice to receive the habit from Newman, and who died on 8 June 1962, aged 96.

The 'Historical' process was then introduced by which the case for Newman's sanctity was to be proved largely by written evidence collected by an historical commission of three experts, only one of which could belong to the same order as the candidate.

In the end, four members of the Historical Commission, not three, were chosen. First of all Archbishop David Matthew, previously Auxiliary of Westminster and Apostolic Delegate to East and West Africa, and at the time Bishop-in-Ordinary to His Majesty's forces and an historical expert on the Stuart period of English history; Father Stephen Dessain of the Birmingham Oratory; Miss Meriol Trevor (who was working on her two-volume biography of the Cardinal); and Jonathan Robinson, a Canadian, then thinking of joining the Birmingham Oratory and now Provost of the Toronto Oratory in Canada. Monsignor H. Francis Davis was made Vice-Postulator, but the Commission never met and its members either died or were dispersed.

All was not lost, however. Meriol Trevor was working on her two-volume biography of Newman,

The Pectoral Cross belonging to Blessed John Henry Newman recovered from his grave at Rednal on 2 October 2008

'The Pillar of the Cloud and Light in Winter'; and Father Stephen Dessain, Archivist and then Provost of the Birmingham Oratory, realising that no true picture of Newman could be gathered without editing Newman's Letters and Diaries, began that monumental task himself. There was in existence a selection of Newman's letters covering his life in the Church of England, so Father Dessain started with Volume XI, October 1845 and continued with this vital work until his sudden death in May 1976, by which time he had covered the whole of Newman's Catholic life, 1845-1890, in 21 volumes.

The brass name-plate from the wooden coffin in which Cardinal Newman was buried, also recovered from his grave

Cardinal Newman's gravestone at the Oratory Retreat, Rednal

This work, one of the most important of its kind in the English language, has been continued by other scholars - the final volume XXXII - the supplementary volume - was published in October 2008. A special dinner was held at Oriel College, Oxford, to mark the completion of the work.

In 1973, something completely unexpected happened. The community at the Oratory House (here) in Edgbaston received an enquiry from Pope Paul VI about the state of the Newman Cause. The Holy Father was interested, if possible, in having Newman beatified during the Holy Year of 1975. Unfortunately, although a great deal of work had been done in editing the 'Letters and Diaries' of Cardinal Newman, which ultimately assisted the Cause, direct work on the Cause was not in a state to allow consideration of Beatification in the Holy Year.

Since Pope Paul VI, a Newman devotee himself, was in favour of Newman's Beatification, it was clear that is was necessary to get the Cause going again by getting the Archbishop of Birmingham to re-appoint the Historical Commission. This proved a longer business than expected, and it was not until 1980 that it eventually got to work.

In the meantime, one or two other vital factors had helped to further Newman's Cause. Mother Julia, the Foundress of a new order in the Church (now the 'Spiritual Family of The Work') had found a 'spiritual brother' in Cardinal Newman. To promote interest in him and his work, she arranged a Newman Symposium in Rome during Easter Week 1975, under the Presidency of Cardinal Wright, Prefect of the Sacred Congregation of the Clergy. This included an arrangement for the choir of St Philip's Grammar School, Birmingham, (run by the Oratory Fathers), to attend and sing at a number of venues including the opening meeting of the Symposium, and at a Mass in St Peter's Basilica.

This Symposium, as we had hoped and prayed, helped to put Cardinal Newman at the forefront of the minds of the Roman Curia and its Cardinals and Bishops, and in the minds of academic and student members of the Roman universities. It was followed up by the events organised in 1979, to mark the Centenary of Newman being made a Cardinal. This included a pilgrimage to Rome led by Bishop Alan Clark of East Anglia and Bishop Joseph Cleary, Auxiliary Bishop of Birmingham. Archbishop Dwyer of Birmingham had planned to go too, but ultimately had to cancel his booking due to other engagements.

Another factor that helped to promote the Cause was the founding of the 'Friends of Cardinal Newman' in 1976. It had become clear that an organisation was necessary to promote popular devotion and collect evidence of it, and to provide people with prayer cards and to which they could write for Newman literature. The inaugural meeting was held at Westminster Cathedral Hall, under the chairmanship of His Grace Miles, (17th) Duke of Norfolk who became President of the new society until his death, in 2002.

The Friends encouraged people to pray continuously for the success of the Cause and assisted the Postulator by reporting instances of devotion and favour granted. It encouraged people worldwide to report Newman's spiritual influence. It collected donations for furthering the Cause and spread knowledge of this Servant of God and his teaching through its newsletter.

Today, there is interest in Newman worldwide, with people from every continent visiting the Birmingham Oratory and seeing the place where Newman wrote many of his famous letters, and lived (from 1852-1890) and where he died on Monday 11 August 1890.

In 1979, after the centenary celebrations of Newman being created a Cardinal by Pope Leo XIII in 1879, the Most Reverend George Patrick Dwyer, Archbishop of Birmingham, agreed to the reconstitution of the Historical Commission and the appointment of a Diocesan Postulator for Newman's Cause.

In 1980, the Archdiocese of Birmingham Historical Commission was reconvened with Father Vincent Ferrer Blehl SJ, as its Chairman, and the Reverend Dr Derek Holmes and Mr Gerard Tracey, Archivist at the Birmingham Oratory, as its three members. Monsignor Anthony Stark, Master of the Guild of Our Lady of Ransom, was appointed the Diocesan Postulator, and he was still Chairman of the Friends of Cardinal Newman at the time of the Beatification of Cardinal Newman.

To the delight of everyone connected with Newman's Cause, after a year of celebrations in 1990 to mark the centenary of Newman's death, on 22 January 1991 Pope John Paul II announced that Newman had practised the heroic virtues.

The Holy Father solemnly declared that: 'It is certain that the Servant of God, John Henry Newman, Cardinal of the Holy Roman Church, and Founder of the Oratory of Saint Philip Neri in England, had practised the theological virtues of Faith, Hope and Charity towards God and his neighbour, also the cardinal virtues of Prudence, Justice, Temperance and Fortitude and those connected with them, to a heroic degree, in accordance with the requirements of the investigation of this case.'

After declaring Newman 'Venerable', Pope John Paul said that it was: 'A most important Cause'.

The Death Certificate of the now Blessed John Henry Newman

The work of the Historical Commission, in gathering thousands of pages of evidence was completed by the summer of 1986 and the Diocesan Process wound up. The evidence was sent to Rome following a special service at the Metropolitan Cathedral and Minor Basilica of St Chad, Birmingham, under the Presidency of the Archbishop, the Most Reverend Maurice Couve de Murville, whose appointment as Archbishop of Birmingham had been announced by the Holy See a few weeks before the Pastoral Visit of Pope John Paul II to Great Britain, in 1982.

Father Blehl was then appointed the Roman Postulator for the next stage of the Cause. Father Blehl completed the Positio, or Case for Cardinal Newman's holiness by February 1989 and it was sent to the Congregation for the Causes of Saints in Rome.

It was the quiet work of Father Blehl that was responsible for the successful assembly of evidence by the Historical Commission, 1980-1986, the meticulous work of compiling the Positio in the following four years, and the subsequent declaration in 1991 that Newman had indeed lived a life of 'heroic virtue'.

It has taken another long period, until 2009, before the necessary 'Miracle' has taken place and been approved, so it was a marvellous occasion when Deacon Jack Sullivan, a permanent deacon from the Archdiocese of Boston, Massachusetts, in the United States of America, came to England in November 2009 to tell us how he had been cured from a crippling spinal condition through Cardinal Newman's intercession.

A MEDITATION BY BLESSED JOHN HENRY NEWMAN

God has created me to do Him some definite service; He has committed some work to me which He has not committed to another. I have my mission - I may never know it in this life, but I shall be told it in the next.

I am a link in a chain, a bond of connection between persons. He has not created me for naught. I shall do good, I shall do His work; I shall be a preacher of truth in my own place, while not intending it, if I do but keep His commandments and serve Him in my calling.

Therefore I will trust Him. Whatever, wherever I am, I can never be thrown away. If I am in sickness, my sickness may serve Him; in perplexity, my perplexity may serve Him; if I am in sorrow, my sorrow may serve Him. My sickness or perplexity or sorrow may be necessary causes of some great end, which is quite beyond us. He does nothing in vain; He may prolong my life, He may shorten it; He knows what he is about. He may take away my friends, He may throw me among strangers, He may make me feel desolate, make my spirits sink, hide my future from me — still He knows what He is about.

WORKERS FOR THE NEWMAN CAUSE

Mgr Anthony Stark, Master of the Guild of Our Lady of Ransom, Diocesan Postulator for the Newman Cause

Ever since the foundation of the 'Friends of Cardinal Newman' the Cause has been a co-operative effort in which people from many institutions connected with Newman have worked together by God's providence in a common cause. For instance, we can think of the support given by the Governors, staff and old boys of the Oratory School founded by Newman at Edgbaston but now at Woodcote near Reading in Berkshire.

Westminster Cathedral, too, played its part through the interest of the Right Reverend Monsignor Gordon Wheeler, Administrator and later Bishop of Leeds; Monsignor Bartlet, Administrator, whose family came from the Oratory Parish in Birmingham, and who built up a huge collection of photographs and slides on all places connected with Newman.

The Newman Association, 'The Work' whose involvement has already been mentioned, and 'The Guild of Ransom' whose Master, the Right Reverend Antony Stark was an old boy of St Philip's Grammar School, in Edgbaston, Birmingham, and educated by the Fathers of the Birmingham Oratory, have worked year by year to promote Cardinal Newman both as a great theologian and writer but also as a practical, pastoral parish priest.

We must not forget the scholars working away in the background and, like Father Ian Ker, producing many books to help us create world-wide interest in Cardinal Newman. The Oxford Oratory, founded in 1990, organised scholarly conferences.

One of the people helping to hold these disparate groups, and others, together, has been Father Gregory Winterton of the Birmingham Oratory who celebrated his 88th birthday in July 2010.

Father Gregory Winterton joined the Birmingham Oratory in 1961, and was ordained a priest during March 1963. Like Cardinal Newman he was a converted Anglican clergyman. He was elected Provost of the Oratory of St Philip Neri, Edgbaston, for the first time on 2 February 1971. Except for an interlude of six months during 1977, he held the office until 2 February 1992, longer than anyone except for Cardinal Newman himself. By virtue of his office as Provost he was also the Actor, or promoter, of the Newman Cause.

Father Gregory helped to revive popular interest in Cardinal Newman by the foundation of 'The Friends of Cardinal Newman' in 1976, and by talks and articles. He continues to edit 'The Friends' informative newsletter usually published twice a year.

The Annual Mass organised by 'The Friends' on 11 August, the anniversary of Newman's death, has been another contributing factor in spreading knowledge and interest in Cardinal Newman for parishes throughout the Archdiocese of Birmingham and beyond. For many years, this Mass was celebrated in the grounds of the Oratory Retreat, Rednal, close to Cofton Park, Birmingham, and was followed by prayers at Newman's graveside. Since it was thought better to have the Mass at the Oratory Church in Edgbaston, a separate service at the graveside has been customary to pray for the Beatification and Canonisation of Cardinal Newman.

Father Gregory Winterton's work on the Newman Cause was publicly recognised when he was chosen to celebrate at the altar close to the Holy Father Pope Benedict XVI, during the Mass for the Beatification of Cardinal Newman.

DEACON JACK SULLIVAN - THE STORY OF A MIRACLE

'Please Cardinal Newman, help me to walk so that I can return to my Diaconate classes and be ordained.'

*J*ack Sullivan's astonishing healing from a crippling spinal condition, now accepted as a miracle by the Roman Catholic Church, took place during Wednesday 15 August 2001, the Feast of the Assumption of Our Blessed Lady.

Jack has retold the amazing story many times: 'This morning the pain was just as intense as the day before. It would come in waves, with intervals about twenty seconds apart, during which I had to adjust my position slightly. The therapist came in earlier than I had anticipated and announced that it was time for my walk.

'I found it excruciatingly painful just to move on to the right side of my bed. Even with the therapist's help it took me more than five minutes. At times I had to stop and catch my breath the pain was so severe; with her help I finally twisted myself over the bed so that my legs touched the cold floor.

'My situation appeared to be hopeless. I silently, but fervently, prayed to Cardinal Newman for his urgent help. I will never forget the simple words that I said that morning: *'Please Cardinal Newman, help me to walk so that I can return to my Diaconate classes and be ordained.'*

'Suddenly, I felt a very warm sensation all over my body. I began to shudder and felt a strong tingling sensation, which gripped my entire body. It lasted for what seemed a long time, and was very strong. Then I felt a surge of strength, confidence and a tremendous sense of peace and joy that I could finally walk, and I was completely free of the crippling pain.

'My healing became remarkably and inexplicably accelerated - two to three months in one moment of time. I smiled, refused the walking aid that I had been given, and for the first time in several months

I was now walking upright, normally, and felt real power and strength in both my legs.

'The therapist was truly amazed and she turned and said: 'Jack, you have passed with flying colours this morning and therefore you can now go back to your room, and I will authorise your discharge from the hospital'. I just wanted to walk and walk. I wanted to walk down to the other end of the corridor where there was a large window, plants, and some chairs, much like an atrium.

'I stood by the windows thrilled by the beautiful scenery. The therapist suggested to me several times that I sit down in an easy chair. I replied that it wasn't necessary, because I was just so delighted to be standing upright, instead of being bent over double. We stood there for about fifteen minutes and then I walked back to my room. The nurse telephoned my wife Carol and asked her to come to the hospital and take me home.

'The head nurse warned me to be extremely careful about bending, turning or twisting. She also told me that I should use a cane when getting up from my bed or a chair. I was given a bottle of painkillers and told to take two, every four hours.

Deacon Jack Sullivan and his wife Carol welcomed to Birmingham on 16 September 2010 by a rainbow, always a sign of God's promise to his people

I took two pills before bed that first night just as a precaution; for I was pain-free.

'From that moment, on the Feast of the Assumption 2001, to this day in 2008, the pain has never once returned and I continue to walk normally with no restrictions to movement and with full mobility.'

The background to this amazing recovery from an extremely serious and crippling spinal disorder is entwined with the experience of excruciating pain.

After many months of waiting, surgery took place on Thursday 9 August 2001. It took longer than anticipated because Jack's lower spine was so badly ruptured.

On Saturday 11 August 2001, the Anniversary of Cardinal Newman's death in 1890, Jack was told to lie in bed perfectly still on his left side in order to allow the incision into the membrane surrounding the spinal cord to heal. Morphine had to be administered every few hours. 'I remember that at the time, my heart was filled with joy and gratitude to Cardinal Newman for seeing me through this difficult surgery.'

On Tuesday 14 August Jack was told that he could not be discharged from hospital until he was able to walk with the aid of a walking stick.

After he had received his medication to relieve the pain, Jack's physiotherapist came and announced that it was time for a walking test. 'The physiotherapist gave me a walking aid and I somehow managed to get out of bed, but after only a short time I had to be helped back onto the bed. I was told that my recovery period would be extended by several weeks; I was demoralised.'

Two days later, on Thursday 16 August, the day after the miracle, the nurse who visited Jack at his home was surprised to find him virtually free from pain. The nurse recommended that he walk for short distances, in his garden, but that he should be careful about bending.

By Sunday 19 August, instead of having Holy Communion brought to him by the Pastoral Associate of St Christine's Parish, in Marshfield, Massachusetts, Jack was able to attend the nine o'clock Mass. The congregation was amazed and astounded to see Jack standing upright and walking normally, as they knew of the severity of his condition and recent surgery. The last time he had entered the church, he was hunched over, with his face looking towards the ground.

Jack began walking further each day without the aid of a walking stick. Within two weeks he was able to walk more than two miles each day, and he has done so ever since. He now feels amazingly fit.

Jack first told his deeply moving and inspirational story, to this author, for the Vatican Congregation for the Cause of Saints, for inclusion in the *Positio Super Miro*: 'Beatification of the Servant of God John Henry Newman, Cardinal of the Holy Roman Church,

Founder of the Oratory of Saint Philip Neri in England (1801-1890).'

Jack added to his account, and it was subsequently published in September 2009, in a CTS booklet: *Cardinal Newman: The Story of a Miracle*, by Peter Jennings. The Most Reverend Vincent Nichols, then Archbishop of Birmingham, wrote the Foreword.

The Cause for the Beatification and Canonisation of Cardinal Newman opened at the Birmingham Oratory in October 1958 but did not make much progress. The Cause was revitalised in the Holy Year of 1975, by Father Gregory Winterton, then Provost of the Birmingham Oratory, after Pope Paul VI had enquired why no progress had been made.

The approval of the miracle of Jack Sullivan's healing by the Congregation for the Causes of Saints, on 2 June 2009, cleared the way for the Beatification of John Henry Newman. The Papal Decree was promulgated by Pope Benedict XVI, a month later, on 3 July 2009.

Four months later, at the invitation of the Most Reverend Vincent Nichols, the Archbishop of Birmingham (by then Archbishop of Westminster), Deacon Jack Sullivan and his wife Carol made a pilgrimage to England, Monday 9 - Sunday 15 November 2009, in order to visit some of the places associated with Newman and to tell his story at specially arranged Masses and events.

Deacon Jack Sullivan spoke about his miracle of healing on three significant public occasions. The first was in Westminster Cathedral on 9 November 2009, the Feast of the Roman Martyrs, when the Most Reverend Vincent Nichols, Archbishop of Westminster, and President of the Bishops' Conference of England and Wales, officially welcomed Jack and Carol Sullivan on their first visit to England.

It was a memorable moment, when Deacon Jack Sullivan walked onto the sanctuary for the five o'clock Sung Mass, holding the Book of the Gospels aloft. The congregation listened intently, as Jack recounted his remarkable story, which was greeted with enthusiastic applause.

Deacon Jack Sullivan pictured in London

The following day, Tuesday 10 November, Jack and Carol were the guests of the Catholic Truth Society, and in the evening, Deacon Jack Sullivan gave the *CTS Lecture 2009 - 'The Story of a Miracle'*, at the London Oratory, which event was attended by more than 500 people.

On Wednesday 11 November Deacon Jack Sullivan was the guest of the Fathers of the Birmingham Oratory, in Edgbaston. Thus, Jack was able to see with his own eyes the places where Cardinal Newman lived for most of his Catholic life, and where he died on Monday 11 August 1890.

Deacon Sullivan gave the homily at the 12:45 pm Mass in the Newman Memorial Church (The Birmingham Oratory), during which he told the story of his miraculous healing, by God, through the intercession of Cardinal John Henry Newman.

Deacon Sullivan ended: 'Thank you Archbishop Vincent Nichols, for inviting me to come home. This is Newman's home: so I am home! God bless you all.'

THE OFFICIAL ANNOUNCEMENT - THE STATE VISIT OF POPE BENEDICT XVI TO THE UNITED KINGDOM

The official announcement of the State Visit of His Holiness Pope Benedict XVI to the United Kingdom was made by Buckingham Palace at noon on 16 March 2010.

At the time, no details of the official programme were given except the news that the Beatification Ceremony of the Venerable John Henry Newman would take place at Coventry Airport on Sunday 19 September 2010, the last day of a four-day visit.

The press briefing, which was relaxed, was hosted by the Right Honourable Jim Murphy MP, Secretary of State for Scotland, at the Foreign and Commonwealth Office. Mr Murphy, a Catholic Member of Parliament, now in opposition, was at the time the Minister leading the preparations for the first State Visit ever to be made by a Pope to the United Kingdom.

During the briefing, the Most Reverend Vincent Nichols, Archbishop of Westminster and President of the Bishops' Conference of England and Wales, emphasised that it would be the first time during his Pontificate that Pope Benedict XVI had beatified any Servant of God.

Since the election of Pope Benedict XVI, in April 2005, all Beatification ceremonies, with a few exceptions in Rome, had been held in the diocese where the Servant of God was either born, lived or died. It was the personal wish of Pope Benedict XVI to come to England and beatify Cardinal Newman in the Archdiocese of Birmingham.

Archbishop Nichols added: 'We are confident that the presence and message of Pope Benedict XVI will encourage everyone to aspire again to a vision of life in our society marked by mutual trust, compassion and truth. The great Christian

tradition of faith and life, which has so shaped our culture, has so much more to offer. This gentle yet profound teacher of his faith will encourage and strengthen all who received his words.'

His Eminence, Keith Patrick, Cardinal O'Brien, Archbishop of St Andrew's and Edinburgh and President of the Bishops' Conference of Scotland, said: 'A defining feature of Pope Benedict's teaching has been to remind Europe of its Christian roots and culture and to give us guidance on the great moral issues of our day. It is my hope that we all open our hearts to the Holy Father's words.'

The Holy See changed the venue for the Beatification from Coventry Airport to Cofton Park, Birmingham, on 24 June 2010, the Feast of Saint John the Baptist. The park, shaped in the form of an amphitheatre, and owned by Birmingham City Council, was considered to be a more suitable venue because of its location close to the Oratory Retreat, Rednal, where Cardinal Newman had been buried in the small secluded community graveyard following his Funeral Mass at the Oratory House, Edgbaston, on Tuesday 19 August 1890.

After the official announcement, The Very Reverend Father Richard Duffield, Provost of the Birmingham Oratory and Actor of the Cause of John Henry Newman, issued the following statement: 'The Fathers and many friends of the English Oratories are delighted by the official announcement that our Holy Father Pope Benedict XVI will beatify our Founder, the Venerable John Henry Newman, in the Archdiocese of Birmingham during his State Visit to the United Kingdom in September 2010.

'Cardinal Newman made his home in the Archdiocese of Birmingham for all his adult life, first in Oxford, where he lived as an Anglican and was received into the Catholic Church, and later in Birmingham itself, where he founded and worked in the Birmingham Oratory for more than forty years.

'The Holy Father's life-long devotion to Newman has made a profound contribution to understanding the depth and significance of our Founder's legacy. His decision to beatify Newman in person confers a unique blessing upon the English Oratories and all who have drawn inspiration from Newman's life and work.'

Father Duffield added: 'We joyfully look forward to welcoming the Holy Father, as well as the many pilgrims and visitors who will come to the Beatification ceremony and visit Newman's shrine at the Birmingham Oratory.'

The United Kingdom and the Holy See recommended diplomatic relations in 1914 and agreed full ambassadorial relations during 1982. This was the year that His Holiness Pope John Paul II made an historic and successful six-day Pastoral Visit to Great Britain, during the Falklands conflict, 28 May - 2 June.

The invitation to the Holy Father, Pope Benedict XVI to undertake a State Visit to the United Kingdom, was made by Her Majesty The Queen following earlier invitations being made by His Royal Highness the Prince of Wales; former Prime Minister the Right Honourable Tony Blair, MP, and the succeeding Prime Minister, the Right Honourable Gordon Brown, MP, Chancellor, during official visits to Pope Benedict XVI in Rome.

During the Queen's Speech in the House of Lords on 25 May 2010, Her Majesty said: 'The Duke of Edinburgh and I look forward to receiving His Holiness Pope Benedict XVI in September.'

Following the General Election, held on Thursday 6 May, the Coalition Government led by the Prime Minister the Right Honourable David Cameron, MP and the Right Honourable Nick Clegg, MP, Deputy Prime Minister assumed responsibility for the State Visit. The Prime Minister, David Cameron, appointed Lord Patten of Barnes, the last Governor of Hong Kong and currently the Chancellor of the University of Oxford, a Catholic, as his personal representative for the State Visit of Pope Benedict XVI to the United Kingdom.

The theme of the State Visit, 'Cor ad Cor Loquitur' - 'Heart Speaks unto Heart', was the motto chosen by Cardinal Newman for his Coat of Arms when he was created Cardinal by Pope Leo XIII, in May 1879. These inspirational words come from the writings of Saint Francis de Sales (1567-1622), Doctor of the Church, Patron Saint of writers and journalists to whom Cardinal Newman had a particular devotion.

POPE BENEDICT XVI LOOKS FORWARD TO HIS VISIT TO THE UNITED KINGDOM

Pope Benedict XVI, during his weekly General Audience on Wednesday 8 September 2010, Feast of the Birthday of Our Lady, in the Paul VI Audience Hall at the Vatican, spoke about his forthcoming State Visit to the United Kingdom.

The Holy Father said: '*I am very much looking forward to my visit to the United Kingdom in a week's time and I send heartfelt greetings to all the people of Great Britain.* I am aware that a vast amount of work has gone into the preparations for the visit, not only by the Catholic community, but by the Government, the local authorities in Scotland, London and Birmingham, and the communications, media and the security services, and I want to say how much I appreciate the efforts that have been made, to ensure that the various events planned will be truly joyful celebrations. Above all, I thank the countless people who have been praying for the success of the visit and for a great outpouring of God's grace upon the Church and the people of your nation.

'It will be a particular joy for me to beatify the Venerable John Henry Newman, in Birmingham, on Sunday 19 September. This truly great Englishman lived an exemplary priestly life and through his extensive writings made a lasting contribution to Church and society both in his native land and in many other parts of the world. It is my hope and prayer that more and more people will benefit from his gentle wisdom and be inspired by his example of integrity and holiness of life.

'I look forward to meeting representatives of the many different religious and cultural traditions that make up the British population, as well as civil and political leaders. I am most grateful to Her Majesty The Queen and to His Grace the Archbishop of Canterbury for receiving me, and I look forward to meeting them. While I regret that there are many places and people I shall not have the opportunity to visit, I want you to know that you are all remembered in my prayers. God bless the people of the United Kingdom.'

'I COME WITH GREAT COURAGE AND JOY'

His Holiness Pope Benedict XVI's mid-flight Press Conference

Thursday 16 September 2010

As is traditional, the Holy Father, Pope Benedict XVI, accompanied by Father Federico Lombardi SJ, Papal Spokesman, held a mid-flight press conference with journalists accompanying him on his four-day State Visit to the United Kingdom.

QUESTION: Your Holiness, during the preparation for this journey there have been contrary discussions and positions. The country has a past tradition of a strong anti-Catholic position. Are you concerned about how you will be received?

POPE BENEDICT XVI: Firstly, good day to you all and I wish you a good journey. I must say that I am not worried, because when I went to France I was told: 'This will be a most anticlerical country with strong anticlerical currents and with a minimum of faithful.' When I went to the Czech Republic it was said: 'This is the most non-religious country in Europe and even the most anti-clerical'. So Western countries, all have, each in their own specific way, according to their own history, strong anticlerical or anti-Catholic currents, but they always also have a strong presence of faith.

So in France and the Czech Republic I saw and experienced a warm welcome by the Catholic community, a strong attention from agnostics, who, however, are searching, who want to know, to find the values that advance humanity and they were very careful to see if they could hear

The Holy Father accompanied by Cardinal Bertone and Fr Frederico Lombardi SJ answering questions from journalists during the flight from Rome to Edinbugh

something from me in this respect, and tolerance and respect for those who are anti-Catholic.

Of course Britain has its own history of anti-Catholicism, this is obvious, but is also a country with a great history of tolerance. And so I'm sure on the one hand, there will be a positive reception from Catholics, from believers in general, and attention from those who seek as we move forward in our time, mutual respect and tolerance. Where there is anti-Catholicism I will go forward with great courage and joy.

QUESTION: Your Holiness, the United Kingdom, like many other Western countries - this is an issue that you have already touched on in the first answer   is considered a secular country. There is a strong atheist movement, even for cultural reasons. However, there are also signs that religious faith, particularly in Jesus Christ, is still alive on a personal level. What can this mean for Catholics and Anglicans? Can anything be done to make the Church as an institution, more credible and attractive to everyone?

POPE BENEDICT XVI: I would say that a Church that seeks to be particularly attractive is already on the wrong path, because the Church does not work for her own ends, she does not work to increase numbers and thus power. The Church is at the service of another: she serves, not for herself, not to be a strong body, rather she serves to make the proclamation of Jesus Christ accessible, the great truths and great forces of love, reconciling love that appeared in this figure and that always comes from the presence of Jesus Christ.

In this regard, the Church does not seek to be attractive in and of herself, but must be transparent for Jesus Christ and to the extent that she is not out for herself, as a strong and powerful body in the world, that wants power, but is simply the voice of another, she becomes truly transparent for the great figure of Christ and the great truth that he has brought to humanity. The power of love, in this moment one listens, one accepts. The Church should not consider herself, but help to consider the other and she herself must see and speak of the other.

In this sense, I think, both Anglicans and Catholics have the same simple task, the same direction to take. If both Anglicans and Catholics see that the other is not out for themselves but are tools of Christ, children of the Bridegroom, as Saint John says, if both carry out the priorities of Christ and not their own, they will come together, because at that time the priority of Christ unites them and they are no longer competitors seeking the greatest numbers, but are united in our commitment to the truth of Christ who comes into this world and so they find each other in a genuine and fruitful ecumenism.

QUESTION: Your Holiness, as is well-known and as was also highlighted by recent surveys, the sexual abuse scandal has shaken the confidence of the faithful in the Church. How do you think you can help restore that trust?

POPE BENEDICT XVI: First, I must say that these revelations have been a shock for me, not only a great sadness. It is difficult to understand how this perversion of the priestly ministry was possible. The priest at the time of ordination, after having prepared for this moment for years, says yes to

Christ, to be his voice, his mouth, his hands and serve Him with his whole life, so that the Good Shepherd who loves and helps and guides to the truth is present in the world. How a man who has done this and said this may also fall into this perversion is difficult to understand.

It is a great sadness, a sadness that even the authority of the Church has not been sufficiently vigilant and not fast or decisive enough in taking the necessary measures. Because of all of this, we are in a time of repentance, humility, and renewed sincerity. As I wrote to the Irish Bishops, I think we now realise it is a time of penance, a time to renew and relearn humility with complete sincerity.

Regarding the victims, I would say there are three important things. Our first interest is for the victims: how can we repair the damage done? What can we do to help these people overcome this trauma, to regain their life and rediscover confidence in the message of Christ? Care, commitment to victims is the first priority, with material, psychological, spiritual aid.

Second, the problem of the guilty persons. The just punishment is exclusion from all possibilities of access to young people because we know that this is a disease and free will does not work where there is disease. So we have to protect these people against themselves and find ways to help them, protect them against themselves and exclude them from any access to young people.

The third point is prevention in education, in the choice of candidates for the priesthood to be so careful that, as much as humanly possible, we exclude future cases. And I would now also like to thank the British Bishops for their attention and co-operation with both the See of Saint Peter and with public bodies. It seems to me that the British Bishops have done a great job in their attention to the sensitivity of the victims and the law and I am very grateful to them for this.

QUESTION: Your Holiness, the figure of Cardinal Newman is obviously very significant. You have made an exception for Cardinal Newman to preside personally over the Beatification. Do you think that his memory will help to overcome divisions between Anglicans and Catholics? What are the aspects of his personality which you would like to give stronger emphasis to?

POPE BENEDICT XVI: Cardinal Newman is mainly, on the one hand, a modern man, who took on all of the problems of modernity, he experienced the problem of agnosticism, the impossibility of knowing God, of believing; a man who throughout his life was on a journey, a journey to let himself be transformed by the truth, in a search of great sincerity and great willingness, to learn more, to find and to accept the path to true life.

This modernity of his inner-being and life points to the modernity of his faith: it is not a faith in the formulas of a bygone age, it is a most personal form of faith, lived, suffered, found through a long process of renewal and conversion. He is a man of great culture who on the one hand participates in our sceptical culture of today, in the question: 'Can we understand something certain about the truth of man, of the human being, or not? And how can we arrive at the convergence of the verisimilitude?'

A man who, on the other hand, with a great knowledge of the culture of the Church Fathers, he studied and renewed the internal genesis of the faith, thus acknowledging his figure and his inner constitution, he is a man of great spirituality, a great humanism, a man of prayer, of a deep relationship with God and a relationship with himself, and therefore also of a deep relationship with the other men of his and our time.

So I would say these three elements: the modernity of his existence, with all the doubts and problems of our existence today, his great culture, knowledge of the great cultural treasures of mankind, his constant quest for the truth, continuous renewal and spirituality: spiritual life, life with God, give this man an exceptional greatness for our time. Therefore, he is a figure of Doctor of the Church for us, for all and also a bridge between Anglicans and Catholics.

LAST QUESTION: Your Holiness, this visit is considered a State Visit - this is how it has been qualified. What does this mean for relations between the Holy See and the United Kingdom? Are there major points of common accord, particularly given the great challenges of today's world?

POPE BENEDICT XVI: I am very grateful to Her Majesty, Queen Elizabeth II, who wanted to give this visit the rank of a State Visit and who expressed the public nature of this visit and also the common responsibility of politics and religion for the future of the continent, for the future of humanity: the large, shared responsibility so that the values that create justice and politics and which come from religion, share the journey in our time. Of course, the fact that legally it is a State Visit, does not make this visit a political matter, because if the Pope is Head of State, this is just an instrument to ensure the independence of his message and public nature of his work as pastor.

In this sense, the State Visit is substantially and essentially a Pastoral Visit, a visit in the responsibility of the faith for which the Supreme Pontiff, the Pope, exists. Of course, the character of a State Visit focuses attention on the converging interests of politics and religion. Politics is essentially designed to ensure justice and with justice, freedom, but justice is a moral value, a religious value, and so faith, the proclamation of the Gospel, connects with politics in justice and here common interests are also born.

Britain has a great experience and a great record in combating the evils of this time, misery, poverty, disease, drugs and all these struggles against misery, poverty, slavery, abuse of man, drugs - are also the goals of the faith, because they are the aims of the humanisation of man, so that the image of God be restored against the destruction and devastation.

Another common task is the commitment to world peace and the ability to live in peace; peace and education establish the virtues that make man capable of peace. And, finally, an essential element of peace is the dialogue of religions, tolerance, openness to one another and this is a deep aim both of Britain, as a society, and of the Catholic faith: to be open to the outside world, open to dialogue, in this way to be open to truth and the common path of humanity and to rediscovering the values that are the foundation of our humanism.

THE CATHOLIC CHURCH IN SCOTLAND

by The Right Reverend Monsignor John McIntyre and Dr Mary McHugh

Saint Columba

A decisive moment in laying the foundations of the Scottish Catholic Church was the marriage of the Scots king Malcolm Canmore in c.1070 to the Saxon princess Margaret. The Church that she founded in Scotland, acknowledged its debt to the saints of the 4th-7th centuries, such as Ninian, Columba, and Kentigern.

Margaret, and the kings of Scots throughout the Middle Ages, brought to Scotland the civilising and evangelising influences of the great European orders of monks and later of friars. To Margaret and her sons is also attributed the medieval diocesan system. Later in the time of William Wallace and Robert Bruce, the Church became associated with Scotland's drive for independent nationhood.

At the end of the 12th century the Papacy declared the Scottish Church a 'special daughter' of the Holy See, precluding English claims to ecclesiastical overlordship. Two archdioceses were created in the 15th century, St Andrews in 1472, and Glasgow in 1492.

By the 16th century the relationship between the Church, the crown, and the papacy was being compromised by the usurping of Church income, by Scottish Kings and of the rights of appointment to high Church positions. This tension came to a head in 1560, when a Scottish parliament made Calvinist belief and practice the law of the land.

After the religious and political upheavals of the 16th century, Scotland came to be regarded by the Church as a missionary territory. The establishment in 1622 by Pope Gregory XV of the Sacred Congregation for the Propagation of the Faith (Propaganda Fidei) was soon followed, in England, by the appointment of the first Vicar-Apostolic, William Bishop, in 1623.

It was not until more than two centuries later on 4 March 1878, that Pope Leo XIII re-established the diocesan hierarchy in Scotland, with the creation of six Sees, and the appointment of diocesan bishops. Between 1947-48, two further dioceses, Motherwell and Paisley, were added to create the eight dioceses of today.

From the late 18th century onwards, a steadily increasing number of Catholics arrived in the industrial cities and counties of Scotland, particularly from Ireland as well as from the Scottish Highlands and Islands. During the 19th and 20th centuries, other immigrants arrived, from Italy, Lithuania, and Poland.

This growing Catholic urban population created a continuing need for more priests, parishes, churches, and schools. Many parishes began with a building which served a dual function, as both chapel and school. Elsewhere permanent and recognisable churches were also erected.

The 1918 Education (Scotland) Act enabled the Catholic voluntary sector to accept the opportunity provided to fully enter the Scottish education system. In the 19th and 20th centuries, religious orders also made a significant contribution to education by helping to staff the parochial schools and establish Catholic colleges for teacher-training. Parishes also fulfilled social and economic roles, including the promotion of parish savings banks, and even football teams.

The presence into the 20th century of religious orders such as the Franciscans and Dominicans are tangible links with the medieval past. Today, hospices and care services continue the long tradition dating back to medieval times.

In more recent times, the Church in Scotland, while continuing to be enriched by the vision of the Second Vatican Council, has suffered with the rest of the Western Church from a lessening of practising membership and of vocations to the priesthood and religious life, and from the pressure of an increasingly secularised society.

Despite this, the Church in Scotland has many things to take pride in – the quality of its schools both in the state and private sector; its parish communities lively in faith, and the readiness with which bishops and others speak out in defence of Christian values.

I encourage the Catholic professionals, politicians and teachers of Scotland never to lose sight of their calling to use their talents and experience in the service of the faith, engaging contemporary Scottish culture at every level.

- Pope Benedict XVI

The Palace of Holyroodhouse

The Palace of Holyroodhouse, where the Holy Father was received by the Queen, is Her Majesty's official residence in Scotland, and is used for a variety of official engagements.

Its origins can be traced back to 1128, when the Abbey of Holyrood was founded by King David I for the Canons of Saint Augustine, and also to house his late mother's relic of the Holy Rood (Holy Cross).

By the mid-15th century Edinburgh was emerging as Scotland's capital and, in keeping with this new status, in 1501 a building described as the King's Palace at Holyrood was commenced by King James IV. Both the Abbey and the Palace witnessed many great events in history including the marriage of King James IV to Princess Margaret Tudor, the sister of King Henry VIII.

The Palace was also the residence of Mary, Queen of Scots after Her Majesty's return from France after the Dauphin's death, and of King James VI before he acceded to the throne of England in 1603. It was also the base for Bonnie Prince Charlie for some time during the 1745 uprising.

The Palace of Holyroodhouse, Edinburgh

*The Holy Father was warmly welcomed to Scotland
by HRH The Duke of Edinburgh and His Eminence
Cardinal O'Brien at the start of his State Visit*

THE GREETING CEREMONY UPON THE FEAST OF SAINT NINIAN AT THE PALACE OF HOLYROODHOUSE

Her Majesty The Queen's Welcome to His Holiness Pope Benedict XVI

12:00 pm Thursday 16 September 2010

Your Holiness,

I am delighted to welcome you to the United Kingdom, and particularly to Scotland, on your first visit as Pope. I recall with great pleasure the memorable pastoral visit of the late Pope John Paul II to this country in 1982. I also have vivid memories of my four visits to the Vatican, and of meeting some of your predecessors on other occasions. I am most grateful to them for receiving, over the years, a number of members of my family with such warm hospitality.

Much has changed in the world during the nearly thirty years since Pope John Paul's visit. In this country, we deeply appreciate the involvement of the Holy See in the dramatic improvement in the situation in Northern Ireland. Elsewhere, the fall of totalitarian regimes across central and eastern Europe has allowed greater freedom for hundreds of millions of people. The Holy See continues to have an important role in international issues, in support of peace and development and in addressing common problems like poverty and climate change.

Your Holiness, your presence here today reminds us of our common Christian heritage, and of the Christian contribution to the encouragement of world peace, and to the economic and social development of the less prosperous countries of the world. We are all aware of the special contribution of the Roman Catholic Church particularly in its ministry to the poorest and most deprived members of society, its care for the homeless and for the education provided by its extensive network of schools.

Religion has always been a crucial element in national identity and historical self-consciousness.

The Pope, The Queen and Duke of Edinburgh enjoy a moment of calm at Holyroodhouse

This has made the relationship between the different faiths a fundamental factor in the necessary co-operation within and between nation states. It is, therefore, vital to encourage a greater mutual, and respectful understanding. We know from experience that through committed dialogue, old suspicions can be transcended and a greater mutual trust established.

I know that reconciliation was a central theme in the life of Cardinal John Henry Newman, for whom you will be holding a Mass of Beatification on Sunday. A man who struggled with doubt and uncertainty, his contribution to the understanding of Christianity continues to influence many. I am pleased that your visit will also provide an opportunity to deepen the relationship between the Roman Catholic Church and the established Church of England and the Church of Scotland.

Your Holiness, in recent times you have said that 'religions can never become vehicles of hatred, that never by invoking the name of God can evil and violence be justified'. Today, in this country, we stand united in that conviction. We hold that freedom to worship is at the core of our tolerant and democratic society.

On behalf of the people of the United Kingdom I wish you a most fruitful and memorable visit.

THE ADDRESS OF THE HOLY FATHER

The Address of His Holiness Pope Benedict XVI

Palace of Holyroodhouse, Edinburgh
12:10 pm Thursday 16 September 2010

Your Majesty,

Thank you for your gracious invitation to make an official visit to the United Kingdom and for your warm words of greeting on behalf of the British people. In thanking Your Majesty, allow me to extend my own greetings to all the people of the United Kingdom and to hold out a hand of friendship to each one.

It is a great pleasure for me to start my journey by saluting the members of the Royal Family, thanking in particular His Royal Highness the Duke of Edinburgh for his kind welcome to me at Edinburgh Airport. I express my gratitude to Your Majesty's present and previous Governments and to all those who worked with them to make this occasion possible, including Lord Patten and former Secretary of State Murphy. I would also like to acknowledge with deep appreciation the work of the All-Party Parliamentary Group on the Holy See, which has contributed greatly to strengthening the friendly relations existing between the Holy See and the United Kingdom.

As I begin my visit to the United Kingdom in Scotland's historic capital city, I greet in a special way First Minister Salmond and the representatives of the Scottish Parliament. Just like the Welsh and Northern Ireland Assemblies, may the Scottish Parliament grow to be an expression of the fine traditions and distinct culture of the Scots and strive to serve their best interests in a spirit of solidarity and concern for the common good.

The name of Holyroodhouse, Your Majesty's official residence in Scotland, recalls the 'Holy Cross' and points to the deep Christian roots that are still present in every layer of British life. The monarchs of England and Scotland have been Christians from very early times and include outstanding saints like Edward the Confessor and Margaret of Scotland.

As you know, many of them consciously exercised their sovereign duty in the light of the Gospel, and in this way shaped the nation for good at the deepest level. As a result, the Christian message has been an integral part of the language, thought and culture of the peoples of these islands for more than a thousand years. Your forefathers' respect for truth and justice, for mercy and charity come to you from a faith that remains a mighty force for good in your kingdom, to the great benefit of Christians and non-Christians alike.

We find many examples of this force for good throughout Britain's long history. Even in comparatively recent times, due to figures like William Wilberforce and David Livingstone, Britain intervened directly to stop the international slave trade. Inspired by faith, women like Florence Nightingale served the poor and the sick and set new standards in healthcare that were subsequently copied everywhere. John Henry Newman, whose Beatification I will celebrate shortly, was one of many British Christians of his age whose goodness, eloquence and action were a credit to their countrymen and women. These, and many people like them, were inspired by a deep faith born and nurtured in these islands.

Even in our own lifetime, we can recall how Britain and her leaders stood against a Nazi tyranny that wished to eradicate God from society and denied our common humanity to many, especially the Jews, who were thought unfit to live.

I also recall the regime's attitude to Christian pastors and religious who spoke the truth in love, opposed the Nazis and paid for that opposition with their lives. As we reflect on the sobering lessons of the atheist extremism of the 20th

The Queen extends a warm welcome to Pope Benedict

The Queen and the Holy Father exchange presents

century, let us never forget how the exclusion of God, religion and virtue from public life leads ultimately to a truncated vision of man and of society and thus to a 'reductive vision of the person and his destiny' (*Caritas in Veritate*, 29).

Sixty-five years ago, Britain played an essential role in forging the post-war international consensus which favoured the establishment of the United Nations and ushered in a hitherto unknown period of peace and prosperity in Europe. In more recent years, the international community has followed closely events in Northern Ireland which have led to the signing of the Good Friday Agreement and the devolution of powers to the Northern Ireland Assembly. Your Majesty's Government and the Government of Ireland, together with the political, religious and civil leaders of Northern Ireland, have helped give birth to a peaceful resolution of the conflict there. I encourage everyone involved to continue to walk courageously together on the

path marked out for them towards a just and lasting peace.

Looking abroad, the United Kingdom remains a key figure politically and economically on the international stage.

Your Majesty's Government and people are the shapers of ideas that still have an impact far beyond the British Isles. This places upon them a particular duty to act wisely for the common good. Similarly, because their opinions reach such a wide audience, the British media have a graver responsibility than most and a greater opportunity to promote the peace of nations, the integral development of peoples and the spread of authentic human rights. May all Britons continue to live by the values of honesty, respect and fair-mindedness that have won them the esteem and admiration of many.

Today, the United Kingdom strives to be a modern and multicultural society. In this challenging enterprise, may it always maintain its respect for those traditional values and cultural expressions that more aggressive forms of secularism no longer value or even tolerate. Let it not obscure the Christian foundation that underpins its freedoms; and may that patrimony, which has always served the nation well, constantly inform the example your Government and people set before the two billion members of the Commonwealth and the great family of English-speaking nations throughout the world.

May God bless Your Majesty and all the people of Your Majesty's realm. Thank you.

Today, the United Kingdom strives to be a modern and multicultural society. In this challenging enterprise, may it always maintain its respect for those traditional values and cultural expressions that more aggressive forms of secularism no longer value or even tolerate. Let it not obscure the Christian foundation that underpins its freedoms; and may that patrimony, which has always served the nation well, constantly inform the example your Government and people set before the two billion members of the Commonwealth and the great family of English-speaking nations throughout the world.

- Pope Benedict XVI

The Queen and Pope Benedict receive bouquets from local young people

EDINBURGH

The Holy Father joyously received in Edinburgh by the people of Scotland

A rare glimpse of Pope Benedict enjoying typical Scottish hospitality

The residence of Cardinal O'Brien in Edinburgh

SAINT NINIAN

The tradition is that Saint Ninian was a Briton, born during the 4th century, possibly in Northern England. It is popularly believed that he travelled to Rome to learn more about the faith, and was welcomed by Pope Saint Damasus (366-384). He undertook many years of study, and was ordained priest and then bishop by Pope Saint Siricius (384-399).

When he returned home, he settled in Southern Scotland, at Whithorn, where he founded his mission. There he built his church, called 'Candida Casa' or White House. He worked among the Britons of the border regions and also among the Picts, in the modern Lothian region and in Fife. As the first known bishop working in Scotland, he occupies a unique place in Scotland's religious history.

In a poignant coincidence, Pope Benedict XVI arrived in Scotland on Saint Ninian's Day, 16 September 2010, and drove down Prince's Street in his Popemobile as the highlight of the Saint Ninian's Day Parade. Children from schools dedicated to Saint Ninian lined the streets and took part in the Parade.

Saint Ninian

Their flags, their clothes, their faces, all full of Saint Andrew's Cross and Saint Ninian's Day

THE VESTMENTS OF CARDINAL NEWMAN ARE SHOWN TO HIS HOLINESS POPE BENEDICT XVI

*V*estments worn on several occasions by Blessed John Henry Newman when he celebrated Mass in the chapel at Abbotsford House, home of Sir Walter Scott, were brought to Edinburgh and shown to Pope Benedict XVI during his visit to Scotland on 16 September 2010.

Cardinal Newman visited Abbotsford in 1852 and again in 1872 as the guest of his friend James Robert Hope Scott who was married to Sir Walter Scott's granddaughter Charlotte. The Cardinal made a gift of the two ornate vestments to Mary Monica, the daughter of the Hope Scott family who owned the house.

The vestments from Abbotsford, near to the River Tweed, at Melrose in the Borders, were loaned to the Archdiocese of St Andrews and Edinburgh especially for the occasion of the visit of His Holiness Pope Benedict to the home of His Eminence Cardinal Keith O'Brien.

Cardinal Keith O'Brien, wearing one of Cardinal Newman's vestments, pictured with Father Gregory Winterton, former Provost of the Birmingham Oratory and Actor of the Newman Cause, during a special Mass held in the chapel at Abbotsford in November 2007.

THE HOLY FATHER CELEBRATES MASS IN GLASGOW

**The Welcome Address to His Holiness
Pope Benedict XVI made by
the Most Reverend Mario Conti
Archbishop of Glasgow**

*Bellahouston Park Glasgow
5:00 pm Thursday 16 September 2010*

Most Holy Father,

Praised *be Jesus Christ!* Welcome to Glasgow, entitled by one of your predecessors '*Specialis Filia Romanae Ecclesiae*' - the Special Daughter of the Roman Church.

Welcome to Scotland, to the whole of which another of your predecessors extended that coveted title. Welcome to the United Kingdom, whose Monarch earlier today in the name of all its citizens welcomed you. We, Holy Father, echo that welcome; we form a community of faith obedient to the Gospel, which has been preached in these islands for over fifteen centuries - before the land to our south became England, and that on which you stand, Scotland.

You come to us on the actual feast of our first-named missionary Saint Ninian, who, according to a reliable tradition, received his education in Rome and came back ordained to proclaim the Gospel of Christ and to establish His Church.

From Rome also came Saint Augustine, sent by Pope Saint Gregory the Great, your predecessor, whose arrival in Kent coincided with the death on the Holy Island of Iona of Saint Columba, who, with his fellow Irish missionaries, evangelised our Scottish Highlands and Islands. Already a British missionary had taken the faith from these shores to those of Ireland, whose citizens recognise in Saint Patrick their great apostle. Monastic life flourished

The moment of Consecration at the Pope's Bellahouston Mass.

in our lands, giving us such great saints as Aidan of Lindisfarne and the Venerable Bede.

Centuries later, at the time of the Reformation, devoted men and women were martyred on account of their faith. In this very city, Saint John Ogilvie was hanged for his allegiance to the Holy See. Holy Father, in addition to Saint Andrew its patron, Scotland holds dear the memory of a saintly queen, Margaret, whose son David revived the ancient bishoprics.

In England, and well beyond, men and women admire Thomas More, Chancellor of the Realm, who suffered death for obedience to his conscience; while another great Englishman whom Your Holiness means to beatify, John Henry Newman, preached on the primacy of a conscience responsive to the truth.

Welcome, Holy Father, to this spot where your venerable predecessor Pope John Paul II challenged us 'for the future to walk hand in hand', and whereby we have created a warmth of friendship with which Christians throughout the United Kingdom embrace you today in your visit to the lands we love and the communities we serve.

Finally, we welcome you, Holy Father, as the Servant of Christ Jesus and the 'Servant of the Servants of God'.

Céad Míle Fáilte: A hundred thousand welcomes!

THE HOMILY BY THE HOLY FATHER

The Homily given by His Holiness Pope Benedict XVI during Mass at Bellahouston Park

5:15 pm Thursday 16 September 2010

Dear Brothers and Sisters in Christ,
'The Kingdom of God is very near to you!' (Lk 10:9).

With these words of the Gospel we have just heard, I greet all of you with great affection in the Lord. Truly the Lord's Kingdom is already in our midst! At this Eucharistic Celebration in which the Church in Scotland gathers around the altar in union with the Successor of Saint Peter, let us reaffirm our faith in Christ's word and our hope — a hope which never disappoints — in his promises! I warmly greet Cardinal O'Brien and the Scottish Bishops; I thank in particular Archbishop Conti for his kind words of welcome on your behalf; and I express my deep gratitude for the work that the British and Scottish Governments and the Glasgow city fathers have done to make this occasion possible.

Today's Gospel reminds us that Christ continues to send His disciples into the world in order to proclaim the coming of His Kingdom and to bring His peace into the world, beginning house by house, family by family, town by town. I have come as a herald of that peace to you, the spiritual children of Saint Andrew and to confirm you in the faith of Saint Peter (cf. Lk 22:32). It is with some emotion that I address you, not far from the spot where my beloved predecessor Pope John Paul II, celebrated Mass nearly thirty years ago with you and was welcomed by the largest crowd ever gathered in Scottish history.

Much has happened in Scotland and in the Church in this country since that historic visit. I note with great satisfaction how Pope John Paul's call to you to walk hand in hand with your fellow Christians has led to greater trust and friendship with the members of the Church of Scotland, the Scottish Episcopal Church and others. Let me encourage you to continue to pray and work with them in building a brighter future for Scotland based upon our common Christian heritage. In today's first reading we heard Saint Paul appeal to the Romans to acknowledge that, as members of Christ's body, we belong to each other (cf. Rom 12:5) and to live in respect and mutual love. In that spirit, I greet the ecumenical representatives who honour us by their presence.

This year marks the 450th anniversary of the Reformation Parliament, but also the 100th anniversary of the World Missionary Conference in Edinburgh, which is widely acknowledged to mark the birth of the modern ecumenical movement. Let us give thanks to God for the promise which ecumenical understanding and co-operation represents for a united witness to the saving truth of God's word in today's rapidly changing society.

Among the differing gifts which Saint Paul lists for the building up of the Church is that of teaching (cf. Rom 12:7).

The preaching of the Gospel has always been accompanied by concern for the word: the inspired word of God and the culture in which that word takes root and flourishes. Here in Scotland, I think of the three medieval universities founded here by the popes, including that of Saint Andrews, which is beginning to mark the 600th anniversary of its foundation. In the last 30 years and with the assistance of civil authorities, Scottish Catholic schools have taken up the challenge of providing an integral education to greater numbers of students, and this has helped young people not only along the path of spiritual and human growth, but also in entering the professions and public life. This is a sign of great hope for the Church, and I encourage the Catholic professionals, politicians and teachers of Scotland never to lose sight of their calling to use their talents and experience in the service of the faith, engaging contemporary Scottish culture at every level.

The evangelisation of culture is all the more important in our times, when a 'dictatorship of relativism' threatens to obscure the unchanging truth about man's nature, his destiny and his ultimate good. There are some who now seek to exclude religious belief from public discourse, to privatise it or even to paint it as a threat to equality and liberty. Yet religion is in fact a guarantee of authentic liberty and respect, leading us to look upon every person as a brother or sister.

For this reason I appeal in particular to you, the lay faithful, in accordance with your baptismal calling and mission, not only to be examples of faith in public, but also to put the case for the promotion of faith's wisdom and vision in the public forum. Society today needs clear voices which propose our right to live, not in a jungle of self-destructive and arbitrary freedoms, but in a society which works for the true welfare of its citizens and offers them guidance and protection in the face of their weakness and fragility. Do

not be afraid to take up this service to your brothers and sisters, and to the future of your beloved nation.

Saint Ninian, whose feast we celebrate today, was himself unafraid to be a lone voice. In the footsteps of the disciples whom our Lord sent forth before him, Ninian was one of the very first Catholic missionaries to bring his fellow Britons the good news of Jesus Christ. His mission church in Galloway became a centre for the first evangelisation of this country. That work was later taken up by Saint Mungo, Glasgow's own patron, and by other saints, the greatest of whom must include Saint Columba and Saint Margaret. Inspired by them, many men and women have laboured over many centuries to hand down the faith to you. Strive to be worthy of this great tradition! Let the exhortation of Saint Paul in the first reading be your constant inspiration: 'Do not lag in zeal, be ardent in spirit, serve the Lord. Rejoice in hope, be patient in suffering and persevere in prayer' (cf. Rom 12:11-12).

I would now like to address a special word to the bishops of Scotland. Dear brothers, let me encourage you in your pastoral leadership of the Catholics of Scotland. As you know, one of your first pastoral duties is to your priests (cf. *Presbyterorum Ordinis*, 7) and to their sanctification. As they are *alter Christus* to the Catholic community, so you are to them. Live to the full the charity that flows from Christ, in your brotherly ministry towards your priests, collaborating with them all, and in particular with those who have little contact with their fellow priests. Pray with them for vocations, that the Lord of the harvest will send labourers to his harvest (cf. Lk 10:2). Just as the Eucharist makes the Church, so the priesthood is central to the life of the Church. Engage yourselves personally in forming your priests as a body of men who inspire others to dedicate themselves completely to the service of Almighty God. Have a care also for your deacons, whose ministry of service is associated in a particular way with that of the order of bishops. Be a father and a guide in holiness for them, encouraging them to grow in knowledge and wisdom in carrying out the mission of herald to which they have been called.

Dear priests of Scotland, you are called to holiness and to serve God's people by modelling your lives on the mystery of the Lord's cross. Preach the Gospel with a pure heart and a clear conscience. Dedicate yourselves to God alone and you will become shining examples to young men of a holy, simple and joyful life: they, in their turn, will surely wish to join you in your single-minded service of God's people. May the example of Saint John Ogilvie, dedicated, selfless and brave, inspire all of you. Similarly, let me encourage you, the monks, nuns and religious of Scotland to be a light on a hilltop, living an authentic Christian life of prayer and action that witnesses in a luminous way to the power of the Gospel.

Finally, I would like to say a word to you, my dear young Catholics of Scotland. I urge you to lead lives worthy of our Lord (cf. Eph 4:1) and of yourselves. There are many temptations placed before you every day - drugs, money, sex, pornography, alcohol - which the world tells you will bring you happiness, yet these things are destructive and divisive.

There is only one thing which lasts: the love of Jesus Christ personally for each one of you. Search for him, know him and love him, and he will set you free from slavery to the glittering but superficial existence frequently proposed by today's society. Put aside what is worthless and learn of your own dignity as children of God. In today's Gospel, Jesus asks us to pray for vocations: I pray that many of you will know and love Jesus Christ and, through that encounter, will dedicate yourselves completely to God, especially those of you who are called to the priesthood and religious life. This is the challenge the Lord gives to you today: the Church now belongs to you!

Dear friends, I express once more my joy at celebrating this Mass with you. I am happy to assure you of my prayers in the ancient language of your country: *Sìth agus beannachd Dhe dhuibh uile; Dia bhi timcheall oirbh; agus gum beannaicheadh Dia Alba.* God's peace and blessing to you all; God surround you; and may God bless the people of Scotland!

I urge you to lead lives worthy of our Lord.

- Pope Benedict XVI

Glimpses, and sounds, from Bellahouston: pipers and drummer,

a throng stretching to the horizon,

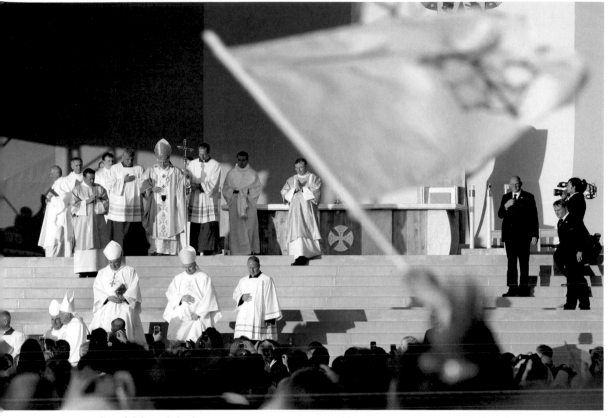

a flag unfurled towards the altar,

and a banner, "Glasgow welcomes Papa Beny", flourished before the advancing Popemobile

HIS HOLINESS POPE BENEDICT XVI IN SCOTLAND - REFLECTIONS

The Most Reverend Mario Joseph Conti, Archbishop of Glasgow

A Reflection on the Mass in Bellahouston Park, Glasgow

Sometimes a day or an event can be defined by a colour. The visit of Pope Benedict this week was one such occasion, and the colour by which I will always remember it is gold.

It was a golden day in every sense ... the Holy Father at the centre, in his beautiful golden mitre and cloth-of-gold vestments; the gold-coloured umbrellas which stretched out through the park marking the spots where priests took communion to people far and near; and that amazing golden glow which settled over the scene as the Mass drew to its close and the sun set in the west at the end of a momentous day.

I felt so privileged to be the one who welcomed the Pope on behalf of the Church to Glasgow, to Scotland and to the United Kingdom. As the Holy Father arrived by car at the space behind the altar, I stepped forward to meet him. It was a private moment but one I will never forget, for the intensity of his look and the sense of peace which he radiated.

As soon as I had arrived at Bellahouston Park, a little ahead of the Pope, I knew that all would be well. The atmosphere was wonderful; happy, prayerful, supportive - all I could have hoped for. Later as we both stood high on that sanctuary in the park, I stepped forward to read my formal message of welcome. I had spent a long time preparing my speech and hoped it would provide a suitable introduction to the Mass and to the visit.

The last few words of Gaelic proved tricky as I bid him a hundred thousand welcomes. But I was amazed to hear the Holy Father himself had been practising Scotland's native tongue to deliver the final message of his sermon, again a sign of his thoughtfulness.

Archbishop Mario Conti

When it was all over, some members of the Papal entourage approached me to say that the Pope had been overwhelmed by how warm a welcome he had received and how well everything had gone. The Holy Father said that it was one of the warmest welcomes he had ever received. It was the final touch to a perfect day.

The Reverend Father Noel Barry, Parish Priest, St Agnes', Lambhill, Glasgow

A Reflection on the Papal Visit to Scotland of 2010 with reference to the Papal Visit made in 1982

From beginning to end, it was all sunshine and smiles. Yet, for all the joyful exuberance which gripped the estimated 65,000 people who began gathering at Glasgow's Bellahouston Park even before Alitalia's 'Shepherd One' landed at Edinburgh Airport - the reverential, prayerful silences before and during the celebration of Mass underlined what really mattered.

Just as the critics and the cynics were confounded by the 125,000 people who celebrated so joyfully when the tartan-clad Pope Benedict travelled along Edinburgh's Princes Street, Bellahouston's autumnal wind and chill simply could not overcome the warmth of fellowship which exemplified the day.

Uplifted by pipe bands, hymn rehearsals led by the 800-strong choir with some unforgettable performances by school children, the enthusiastic cheering and waving of flags and banners signalled the appreciative sincerity of the Scottish welcome when the Pope finally arrived.

Comparisons with Pope John Paul's day at Bellahouston in 1982 were inevitable, of course, but somewhat irrelevant. This, after all, was a different Pope, with a different style, and with his own priorities for a different age, highlighted by the polite, purposeful delivery of a homily saturated with wisdom, and oozing with challenges which struck a chord with so many by expressing the caring anxieties of a shepherd very much focused on today's practical and pressing needs.

There was also a conspicuously different political estimation of the occasion, with First Minister Alex Salmond capturing the mood of the pilgrims by declaring himself 'proud' to be there.

Significantly, too, he said something which no Scottish politician was ever likely to admit way back in 1982, by generously acknowledging that 'without the Catholic Church there would have been no Scotland as a country in its own right'.

A day to relish and remember, this was a ten-hour Papal Visit with the promising potential for a deeper and more long-lasting re-energising impact which even the most optimistic could hardly have imagined when Saint Ninian's Day 2010 dawned.

Liz Leydon, Editor of the Scottish Catholic Observer newspaper

A Reflection on the events that took place in Edinburgh for the Saint Ninian's Day Parade and at Bellahouston Park, Glasgow, for the Papal Mass

As the Alitalia plane took off from Birmingham International Airport on Sunday 19 September 2010, the futility of choosing one defining moment or message as the legacy of His Holiness Pope Benedict XVI's visit to our shores began to hit home.

The myriad of events, homilies and speeches in the first ever State Visit to the United Kingdom by a successor of Saint Peter, each deserves a book in its own right, from the historical precedents of a State Visit beginning in Scotland, with a Pontiff entering Westminster Palace and Westminster Abbey, to the Beatification of Cardinal John Henry Newman at Cofton Park.

There is no doubt, however, that the first day of the Papal Visit in Scotland set the tone and turned the tide of apparent negativity in society at large towards the 2010 Visit.

I was personally privileged to see the Holy Father arrive in Edinburgh to bright sunshine and witnessed the warmth of the reception he received there, which rapidly turned to joy as he greeted the crowds gathered for the Saint Ninian's Day Parade accompanied by Cardinal Keith O'Brien. They were both wearing scarves made of the Papal Visit tartan.

While Pope Benedict's words in Edinburgh on the dangers of secularism and 'atheist extremism' struck home, my lasting memory will be hearing his hard-hitting message to Scotland's young Catholic pilgrims during the hauntingly beautiful Bellahouston Mass in Glasgow.

The Holy Father told the young people that in spite of the temptations of the modern world: 'There is only one thing which lasts: the love of Jesus Christ.'

I shared the joy of pilgrims in knowing Pope Benedict better and, in that moment, returned to the child I was in 1982, when his predecessor Pope John Paul II visited and named Scotland the 'Special Daughter of the Roman Church' - a memory Archbishop Conti of Glasgow highlighted in his address of welcome at Bellahouston Park.

THE CATHOLIC CHURCH IN ENGLAND & WALES

From Past to Present: The Presence in England of the Catholic Church

by Madeleine Beard

The mysterious presence of Christianity in Britain reaches back as far as the end of the 2nd century, when the Roman Empire stretched from the shores of the Mediterranean to the North Sea.

The evangelisation of Britain from Rome itself began in 597, when Saint Augustine, accompanied by a number of monks, arrived in Kent and the preaching of the Gospel began. The word mission derives from the final words of the Mass: '*Ite Missa Est*', meaning 'Go forth on your mission'. Moreover, the Celebrant during the Mass, when he reads the Gospel, turns to the North in the sanctuary in recognition of the pagan lands of the north.

So too, today, Pope Benedict, like Pope Saint Gregory the Great before him, turns his attention to England, knowing of its urgent need for re-evangelisation once more. The Gregorian Chant, named after Pope Saint Gregory and today sung in our monasteries, convents and churches, reminds us that what was true in 597 remains true just over 1400 years later. Despite outward appearances, the True Faith proclaimed by the Successor of Saint Peter the Apostle, remains the same.

As Saint Augustine's mission grew, the centuries that followed in England produced many saints that we revere today, after whom so many of our churches are named: Saint Alban, Saint Boniface, Saint Thomas of Canterbury; the monk, Saint David and the Abbess, Saint Hilda; the Prior, Saint John of Bridlington; the historian, Bede the Venerable; the scholar, Saint Edmund of Abingdon and the King, Saint Edward the Confessor. All these and many more ensured that Britain became to be known as the 'Isle of Saints'. Pilgrimages to pray at the shrines which housed their relics were undertaken by many Catholics. Saints' days were celebrated as holy days.

The statue from the shrine of Our Lady of Walsingham

Pilgrimages were undertaken throughout Europe, to Jerusalem, Rome, Santiago and in England to Walsingham in East Anglia, following an apparition in 1061 - the Milky Way was then known as the Walsingham Way. Thus this devotion to the Mother of God prompted the description of England as the 'Dowry of Mary'. Nine hundred and fifty years later, Catholics from throughout Britain still make pilgrimages to this ancient shrine, where King Henry VIII was the last English king to pray.

Over time, the English Catholic Church's strong connection with Rome was emphasised by the sending of a voluntary gift of money to support the Bishop of Rome. Today, this donation, known as 'Peter's Pence', is collected by the Catholic Church worldwide. Indeed, Pope Adrian IV (1154-1159), was the only English Pope who would have been helped in this way by his own countrymen.

The universal devotion of the brown scapular, traditionally worn by Catholics as a form of spiritual protection and incorporated into all monastic habits, was first given to the Carmelite Saint Simon Stock in England in 1251.

Monasteries were at the centre of community life, power-houses of prayer which also provided help for the poor, employment and shelter. The monastic rule, originated by Saint Benedict, was a powerful tool of stability and evangelisation and recognised by Pope Benedict XVI himself by the choice of this name for his pontificate, knowing of the need for the re-evangelisation of Europe. When, at the beginning of the 16th century, the monasteries were destroyed, this sudden breaking of ties with Rome that began with Henry VIII started a turbulent period of immense dislocation, hardship and rupture. The Isle of Saints became the Isle of Martyrs, Saint John Fisher and Saint Thomas More being the most well-known.

Catholics suffered greatly under the Penal Laws introduced against them, with heavy fines and taxes for refusal to attend the services of the Church of England. Those who refused to conform and continued to practise their Catholic Faith became known as 'recusants'. Catholicism went underground and English priests were trained in colleges throughout Europe. The charge of treason was brought against any priest who crossed the Channel from the continent and was brought against any person in England who harboured priests.

Nevertheless, some Catholics took the great risk of helping priests who continued to exercise their

The grim procedure of hanging, drawing and quartering at Tyburn

ministry of administering to the souls of those who still practised the Catholic religion in secret.

It was a very long time before Catholics could legally practise their religion freely again. Towards the end of the 18th century, a few laws changing their status began to be passed but it was the Catholic Emancipation Act (1829) that gave them back equal rights with other subjects, except that of holding the highest offices in the land (which arguably still holds true today).

In the middle of the 19th century, things began to look up. During the summer of 1848, the moves towards the restoration of Catholic bishops with full ecclesiastical authority in England took shape. Pope Pius IX set out a system of Catholic Dioceses in England and Wales in 1850. The former Bishops Apostolic became bishops in their own right. Two years later, Father John Henry Newman was invited to preach at the First Synod of Westminster, held at St Mary's College, Oscott. This gathering marked the formal reinstitution of the Catholic episcopate in England since the break with Rome. The 1852 Synod was a significant moment in the triumphant revival of Catholic life. Newman's role in this sealed his public reputation in the eyes of the Catholic Hierarchy.

Holbein's study of Saint Thomas More

Little did Newman know how prophetic his words were to be. During the next hundred years numerous cathedrals, churches, monasteries, convents and schools were built, funded by generous donations from the Catholic community at home and abroad. These were to be the springboard of a revival of the spread of Catholicism in England during the 19th and 20th centuries.

It is only since the second half of the 20th century that any Pope has voluntarily travelled much beyond Italy. Since Pope Saint Gregory the Great sent Saint Augustine on his mission to these shores in 597, no Pope visited England. But in the Spring of 1982, 140 years after Newman's 'Second Spring' sermon, Pope John Paul II landed not far from Kent, at the start of his historic six-day Pastoral Visit to the Catholic Church in Great Britain. The presence of Pope John Paul II in England, Scotland and Wales captured the imagination of both Catholics and non-Catholics who, to the surprise of many, turned out in their hundreds of thousands to greet him at the great public events or to catch a glimpse of him as he was driven past.

In September 2010, more than twenty-eight years later, Pope Benedict XVI made an historic State Visit to the United Kingdom at the invitation of Her Majesty The Queen and the British Government. A new era of co-operation between the Catholic Church and the State has begun.

Pope John Paul II with The Queen at Buckingham Palace during his Pastoral Visit

Newman's sermon called 'The Second Spring', delivered in the College Chapel on 7 July 1852, is recognised as one of the most important that he preached as a Catholic. In it Newman declared that with the restoration of the Catholic hierarchy was the 'coming of a Second Spring', a new time of abundant growth for the Catholic Church in England and Wales as the Church emerged from the darkness and oppression of penal times.

*A*s I speak to you in this historic setting, I think of the countless men and women down the centuries who have played their part in the momentous events that have taken place within these walls and have shaped the lives of many generations of Britons, and others besides. In particular, I recall the figure of Saint Thomas More, the great English scholar and statesman*

- Pope Benedict XVI

THE ARRIVAL OF CHRISTIANITY IN ENGLAND

The important role played by Monks in the Development of Christianity in England

by Abbot Cuthbert Johnson, OSB

Saint Benedict of Nursia

The importance of the role which monks played in the development of Christianity in England cannot be overestimated. Christianity came to Britain from two directions, both from the north and from the south. Celtic monks came from Ireland to Iona and also to Lindisfarne in Northumbria. To inaugurate the mission, Saint Augustine and a group of monks were sent from Rome by Pope Saint Gregory the Great in 597. They began their missionary work in the south east, Kent being their initial mustering point, as it had been for the Romans before them.

Not only did monks oversee the laying of the foundations of the Church, but they also nurtured and developed both the spiritual and social life of the people, in various parts of the country. The list of names of those who at that time taught the love of God, the love of learning, and who preached the Gospel, is impressive. Of the holy men and women that readily come to mind are Aidan, Cuthbert, Bede, Chad, Wilfred, Hilda and Etheldreda, to name but a few.

The small group of monks who came from Glastonbury to Westminster in 960, at the request of the monk bishop Saint Dunstan (who had been Abbot at Glastonbury) were already the heirs of a great and noble tradition. However, they could not have imagined that from relatively modest and humble beginnings, their Abbey on the banks of the river Thames would develop into one of the most important monastic centres, both in England and also in Europe.

The monks lived their daily lives according to the Rule of Saint Benedict. This Rule, already tried and tested for four centuries, ensured that the monks led a life totally dedicated to God. The monk's day was to be divided between the praise of God in Divine Worship, and the undertaking of sacred reading and work. Each day, the monks gathered seven times in the Abbey Church, in order to sing the Divine Praise and also to celebrate Holy Mass.

The spiritual character of the place and its prestige was enhanced in 1161, when the holy King Edward I was canonised and the shrine in the Abbey Church which housed his relics thus became a place of pilgrimage. Although the element of pilgrimage is little associated with the Abbey, in the minds of many the edifice represents a national shrine and embodies and also contains much which recalls the nation's history.

Perhaps above all, the Abbey is known as the church in which the kings and queens of England are crowned. This association dates back to 1066 when William the Conqueror ascended the throne and was crowned king in the Abbey. Ever since that

13th century manuscript illumination depicting the deposition of the body of King Edward the Confessor in 1066

time, the Abbey has been the sacred place reserved for the coronation of the monarch, and also the setting for other important religious events, composing the pattern of life and death of the Sovereign and that of the wider Royal Family.

The building of the present Abbey Church was begun in 1245, during the reign of King Henry III and it was intended that it should rival, if not surpass, many of the great English and European cathedrals of the period. A sumptuous new shrine was built for the relics of the sainted King Edward the Confessor, which helped not only to enhance the honour of the Saint, but also to enrich the Abbey, through the offerings of numerous pilgrims.

The Rule of Saint Benedict already gave first place in the life of the monk to the celebration of the Sacred Liturgy, but at Westminster Abbey, Divine Worship was celebrated by the monks with a degree of splendour and solemnity appropriate both to the character of the Abbey as a place of pilgrimage and to its relationship with the monarch, until the dissolution of this monastery, and others, by King Henry VIII in 1540, brought this early type of ritual to an end.

The monastic community was dispersed and for sixteen years the chanting of psalms, hymns and canticles of praise by monks was forbidden; until the accession of Queen Mary I, when Catholicism was restored to England, and Westminster Abbey was for a brief space of time re-established as a monastic house.

A former monk of Evesham Abbey, John Feckenham, was appointed Abbot and with a small group of monks he took possession of the Abbey on 21 November, 1556. However, the restoration of monastic life to the ancient Abbey was unable to recapture its former glory and a few months later, on 12 July 1559, after the death of Queen Mary, the Abbey of St Peter's Westminster was once again suppressed.

Queen Mary's successor, Queen Elizabeth I, established the Abbey as a Collegiate Church in 1560 and subsequently as a Royal Peculiar, under the personal jurisdiction of the Sovereign. The Abbey thus continued its role as a place of worship, while reinforcing its special relationship to the Crown.

Although the monastic liturgy ceased, the tradition of daily worship in the Abbey did not.

Over the centuries, many renowned musicians have been associated with the Abbey and have contributed to building up a musical heritage which is still valued today. The Abbey choir and its choir school enjoy worldwide esteem, both for its work and its highly professional standard.

In 1976, a Benedictine monk and abbot became Archbishop of Westminster, leading to a significant ecumenical event. On the early evening of his ordination and installation as Archbishop of Westminster, George Basil Hume OSB (later conferred a Member of the Order of Merit by Her Majesty the Queen) joining together with the Benedictine monks of his former community of Ampleforth, solemnly processed to Westminster Abbey. Here, for the first time in four hundred years, the chant of monastic vespers was heard to resound in the vaults of the Abbey Church. That historic occasion took place on 25 March 1976, upon the Feast of the Annunciation of the Blessed Virgin Mary.

Another event of immense significance took place six years later, during 1982, when the recently elected Pope John Paul II made a Pastoral Visit to Great Britain; though his gruelling schedule sadly did not permit a visit to Westminster Abbey.

Pope John Paul and the Archbishop of Canterbury, the Most Reverend Dr Robert Runcie, took part in an historic and memorable 'Celebration of Faith' in Canterbury Cathedral, the Mother Church of the world-wide Anglican Communion. At the end of the service, the Pope and the Archbishop knelt together in silent prayer, at the site of the martyrdom of Saint Thomas Becket, the Archbishop of Canterbury who had been murdered by the knights of King Henry II, on 29 December 1170.

The visit of Pope Benedict XVI to Westminster Abbey during the State Visit is of great significance. Pope Benedict prayed at the Grave of the Unknown Warrior and also at the Shrine of Saint Edward the Confessor. Pope Benedict and the Archbishop of Canterbury, the Most Reverend Dr Rowan Williams, then addressed the congregation. This was the single ecumenical event of the four-day State Visit of Pope Benedict XVI and represents a most historic occasion in the life of Christianity in 21st-century Britain.

Archbishop Runcie with Pope John Paul II at Canterbury Cathedral in 1982

A CELEBRATION OF CATHOLIC EDUCATION

The Right Reverend Malcolm McMahon, Bishop of Nottingham welcomes His Holiness Pope Benedict XVI to the 'Big Assembly'

St Mary's University College, Twickenham
11:00 am Friday 17 September 2010

Your Holiness Pope Benedict,

It is my honour to welcome you to this celebration of Catholic Education in England, Scotland and Wales. You can see for yourself what great joy your visit brings to our hearts.

Today, we celebrate the many generations of young people who were educated in Catholic schools and colleges and have subsequently taken their place in society to serve the common good.

We celebrate the wonderful sense of faith and community that characterises our schools. And we celebrate with you our faith, our love, and our hope for the future.

At the heart of Catholic Education is our understanding that young people shall have life and have it to the full. That is our theme today.

Christ's words guide us as we strive to educate our children, because we believe that true fulfilment of the human person can only come through a close friendship with Christ.

All that happens in Catholic Education is based on our belief that a human person is made in the image of God and this is most fully expressed in the desire to know and to love.

By educating children and expanding each one's capacity for love, we develop the whole person, nurturing body, spirit and mind alike.

Today, one in ten young people is educated at one of England's 2,200 Catholic schools, with many more in Scotland and Wales. Thousands more young and mature students receive further and higher education in our colleges.

Holy Father, this 'Big Assembly' celebrates some of the powerful forces which connect the students, schools and colleges, and help people live life to the

Happy faces. "Bless you, my dear daughter!" A special moment for one little pilgrim at the 'Big Assembly'

full. These unifying themes include: community, friendship, sport and of course faith.

Such fulfilled lives are only made possible through the relationship between State and Church. Our unique relationship with our government, which we value very much, has enabled Catholic schools and university colleges to make an enormous contribution to the life of our society.

We are also assisted by many members of staff and governors who are not Catholics, but who subscribe to the ethos of Catholic education. In your presence, Holy Father, I thank them on behalf of the Catholic Community.

Our schools and colleges are also integrated into parish communities, local authorities and school networks. A sense of these connections can be felt today with so many children from so many schools and boroughs coming together to greet you, Holy Father, at this 'Big Assembly'.

They are far from alone: through the internet and television, this event is being attended by young people, their families and parish communities, throughout the world - coming together to celebrate this occasion with you. Each person will remember this day for years to come and you can be assured, Holy Father, that they will remember you in their prayers as you continue your visit to the United Kingdom.

And finally, I want to announce that following your historic visit in England and Wales, we'll be celebrating a year of Catholic education, and this will recognise past achievements, but also look forward to a future where we ensure that only the best education is delivered to our young people.

Holy Father, welcome to the 'Big Assembly'.

AN ADDRESS BY THE HOLY FATHER

His Holiness Pope Benedict XVI addresses Teachers and Religious

Chapel of St Mary's University College, Twickenham 11:30 am Friday 17 September

Your Excellency the Secretary of State for Education, Bishop Stack, Dr Naylor, Reverend Fathers, Brothers and Sisters in Christ,

I am pleased to have this opportunity to pay tribute to the outstanding contribution made by religious men and women in this land to the noble task of education. I thank the young people for their fine singing, and I thank Sister Teresa for her words. To her and to all the dedicated men and women who devote their lives to teaching the young, I want to express sentiments of deep appreciation. You form new generations not only in knowledge of the faith, but in every aspect of what it means to live as mature and responsible citizens in today's world.

As you know, the task of a teacher is not simply to impart information or to provide training in skills intended to deliver some economic benefit to society; education is not and must never be considered as purely utilitarian. It is about forming the human person, equipping him or her to live life to the full – in short it is about imparting wisdom. And true wisdom is inseparable from knowledge of the Creator, for 'both we and our words are in his hand, as are all understanding and skill in crafts' (Wis 7:16).

This transcendent dimension of study and teaching was clearly grasped by the monks who contributed so much to the evangelisation of these islands. I am thinking of the Benedictines who accompanied Saint Augustine on his mission to England, of the disciples of Saint Columba who spread the faith across Scotland and Northern England, of Saint David and his companions in Wales. Since the search for God, which lies at the heart of the monastic vocation, requires active engagement with the means by which he makes

Pope Benedict processes into St Mary's Chapel in St Mary's University College

of the young. This gives me an opportunity to give thanks to God for the life and work of the Venerable Mary Ward, a native of this land whose pioneering vision of apostolic religious life for women has borne so much fruit. I myself as a young boy was taught by the 'English Ladies' and I owe them a deep debt of gratitude. Many of you belong to teaching orders that have carried the light of the Gospel to far-off lands as part of the Church's great missionary work, and for this too I give thanks and praise to God. Often you laid the foundations of educational provision long before the State assumed a responsibility for this vital service to the individual and to society. As the relative roles of Church and State in the field of education continue to evolve, never forget that religious have a unique contribution to offer to this apostolate, above all through lives consecrated to God and through faithful, loving witness to Christ, the supreme Teacher.

Indeed, the presence of religious in Catholic schools is a powerful reminder of the much-discussed Catholic ethos that needs to inform every aspect of school life. This extends far beyond the self-evident requirement that the content of the teaching should always be in conformity with Church doctrine. It means that the life of faith needs to be the driving force behind every activity in the school, so that the Church's mission may be served effectively, and the young people may discover the joy of entering into Christ's 'being for others' (*Spe Salvi*, 28).

Before I conclude, I wish to add a particular word of appreciation for those whose task it is to ensure that our schools provide a safe environment for children and young people. Our responsibility towards those entrusted to us for their Christian formation demands nothing less. Indeed, the life of faith can only be effectively nurtured when the prevailing atmosphere is one of respectful and affectionate trust. I pray that this may continue to be a hallmark of the Catholic schools in this country.

With these sentiments, dear Brothers and Sisters, I invite you now to stand and pray.

himself known – his creation and his revealed word – it was only natural that the monastery should have a library and a school (cf. Address to representatives from the world of culture at the '*Collège des Bernardins*' in Paris, 12 September 2008). It was the monks' dedication to learning as the path on which to encounter the Incarnate Word of God that was to lay the foundations of our Western culture and civilisation.

Looking around me today, I see many apostolic religious, whose charism includes the education

His Holiness Pope Benedict XVI addresses Pupils

Sports Arena of St Mary's University College, Twickenham 11:45 am Friday 17 September 2010

Dear Brothers and Sisters in Christ,
Dear young friends,

First of all, I want to say how glad I am to be here with you today. I greet you most warmly, those who have come to St Mary's University from Catholic schools and colleges across the United Kingdom, and all who are watching on television and via the internet. I thank Bishop McMahon for his gracious welcome, I thank the choir and the band for the lovely music which began our celebration, and I thank Miss Bellot for her kind words on behalf of all the young people present. In view of London's forthcoming Olympic Games, it has been a pleasure to inaugurate this Sports Foundation, named in honour of Pope John Paul II, and I pray that all who come here will give glory to God through their sporting activities, as well as bringing enjoyment to themselves and to others.

It is not often that a Pope, or indeed anyone else, has the opportunity to speak to the students of all the Catholic schools of England, Wales and Scotland at the same time. And since I have the chance now, there is something I very much want to say to you. I hope that among those of you listening to me today there are some of the future saints of the 21st century. What God wants most of all for each one of you is that you should become holy. He loves you much more than you could ever begin to imagine, and he wants the very best for you. And by far the best thing for you is to grow in holiness.

Perhaps some of you have never thought about this before. Perhaps some of you think being a saint is not for you. Let me explain what I mean. When we are young, we can usually think of people that we look up to, people we admire, people we want to be like. It could be someone we meet in our daily lives that we hold in great esteem. Or it could be someone famous. We live in a celebrity culture, and young people are often encouraged to model themselves on figures from the world of sport or entertainment. My question for you is this: what are the qualities you

The Holy Father addresses students from Catholic schools and colleges from across the United Kingdom

see in others that you would most like to have yourselves? What kind of person would you really like to be?

When I invite you to become saints, I am asking you not to be content with second best. I am asking you not to pursue one limited goal and ignore all the others. Having money makes it possible to be generous and to do good in the world, but on its own, it is not enough to make us happy. Being highly skilled in some activity or profession is good, but it will not satisfy us unless we aim for something greater still. It might make us famous, but it will not make us happy. Happiness is something we all want, but one of the great tragedies in this world is that so many people never find it, because they look for it in the wrong places. The key to it is very simple — true happiness is to be found in God. We need to have the courage to place our deepest hopes in God alone, not in money, in a career, in worldly success, or in our relationships with others, but in God. Only he can satisfy the deepest needs of our hearts.

Not only does God love us with a depth and an intensity that we can scarcely begin to comprehend, but he invites us to respond to that love. You all know what it is like when you meet someone interesting and attractive, and you want to be that person's friend. You always hope they will find you interesting and attractive, and want to be your friend. God wants your friendship. And once you enter into friendship with God, everything in your life begins to change. As you come to know him better, you find you want to reflect something of his infinite goodness in your own life. You are attracted to the practice of virtue. You begin to see greed and selfishness and all the other sins for what they really are, destructive and dangerous tendencies that cause deep suffering and do great damage, and you want to avoid falling into that trap yourselves. You begin to feel compassion for people in difficulties and you are eager to do something to help them. You want to come to the aid of the poor and the hungry, you want to comfort the sorrowful, you want to be kind and generous. And once these things begin to matter to you, you are well on the way to becoming saints.

In your Catholic schools, there is always a bigger picture over and above the individual subjects you study, the different skills you learn. All the work you do is placed in the context of growing in friendship with God, and all that flows from that friendship. So you learn not just to be good students, but good citizens, good people. As you move higher up the school, you have to make choices regarding the subjects you study, you begin to specialise with a view to what you are going to do later on in life. That is right and proper. But always remember that every subject you study is part of a bigger picture. Never allow yourselves to become narrow. The world needs good scientists, but a scientific outlook becomes dangerously narrow if it ignores the religious or ethical dimension of life, just as religion becomes narrow if it rejects the legitimate contribution of science to our understanding of the world. We need good historians and philosophers and economists, but if the account they give of human life within their particular field is too narrowly focused, they can lead us seriously astray.

A good school provides a rounded education for the whole person. And a good Catholic school, over and above this, should help all its students to become saints. I know that there are many non-Catholics studying in the Catholic schools in Great Britain, and I wish to include all of you in my words today. I pray that you too will feel encouraged to practise virtue and to grow in knowledge and friendship with God alongside your Catholic classmates. You are a reminder to them of the bigger picture that exists outside the school, and indeed, it is only right that respect and friendship for members of other religious traditions should be among the virtues learned in a Catholic school. I hope too that you will want to share with everyone you meet the values and insights you have learned through the Christian education you have received.

Dear friends, I thank you for your attention, I promise to pray for you, and I ask you to pray for me. I hope to see many of you next August, at the World Youth Day in Madrid. In the meantime, may God bless you all!

"We're all here to see the Pope, and we're very happy!"

A REFLECTION ON CATHOLIC EDUCATION

Dr Arthur Naylor,
Principal of St Mary's University College

A Reflection on the Pope's visit to St Mary's University College, Twickenham.

Pope Benedict XVI's visit was quite simply the greatest occasion in the University College's long history. St Mary's was established 160 years ago to train teachers for Catholic schools. The early generations of Simmarians (students and former students of St Mary's) helped to lay the foundations of the Catholic school system, as we know it, and today their successors are to be found teaching in schools across the country and far beyond these shores.

It was a tremendous privilege, therefore, to host the 'Big Assembly' which brought together 4,000 young people and their teachers from schools and colleges across the United Kingdom, for a celebration of the fullness of education, in the presence of the Holy Father. We were joined, through technology, by pupils in every Catholic school in the land which made it genuinely the largest school assembly there has ever been.

The Holy Father's message was beautifully crafted for young people, inviting them to become saints and reminding them where true happiness is to be found.

Earlier, in our University College Chapel, Pope Benedict met and prayed with representatives of religious congregations and orders, particularly those with a charism in Education. The Holy Father recalled his own school days and the influence of the religious sisters, the 'English Ladies', who taught him, and he also reaffirmed the vital importance of schools in the mission of the Church.

My own reflection on the day was how wonderful it had been that so many of our staff from different backgrounds, and across all areas of the University College, together with our student leaders, had been involved in the preparation and organisation of the visit. How much it had meant to each of them to be there on that very special day.

Christ's words guide us as we strive to educate our children, because we believe that true fulfilment of the human person can only come through a close friendship with Christ.

- Pope Benedict XVI

THE MEETING WITH RELIGIOUS LEADERS AND PEOPLE OF FAITH

The Most Reverend Patrick Kelly, Archbishop of Liverpool welcomes His Holiness Pope Benedict XVI to the inter-religious gathering

The Waldegrave Drawing Room, St Mary's University College, Twickenham 12:30 pm, Friday 17 September 2010

Most Holy Father,

When I remember His Holiness, I find that I give ever greater thanks to God for your predecessor, *Pope Paul VI, who referred to this land as a 'terreno ecumenico' - an ecumenical land.*

The story of this land, including the fact that blood was once shed because of conflicts about the way of life in Christ, now offers specific challenges and opportunities in the ecumenical journey to which the Holy Spirit calls us in our day. To that journey, in all its complexity, you are devoting time in this coming part of this day.

But it seems to me that because of our complex history, again with dark days and indeed blood shed through issues of domination, culture, race and religion, I feel this is a unique terrain in an aspect of life across today's world, which gathers us all here today.

There are specific challenges and opportunities which we have had to face and still face, if we would discern together how to be always and everywhere instruments of justice and peace.

We thank you, and I do so in great confidence in the light of the sharing that's taken place here this morning. We thank you for your presence and your words. And we promise that we will be faithful to the ways of truth, wisdom, holiness and peace.

Archbishop Patrick Kelly introduces the Holy Father

The Right Honourable Lord Sacks, Chief Rabbi of the United Hebrew Congregations of the Commonwealth, an Address to His Holiness Pope Benedict XVI

The Waldegrave Drawing Room, St Mary's, Twickenham 12:38 pm Friday 17 September 2010

We welcome you, the Leader of a great Faith, to this gathering of many faiths, in a land where once battles were fought in the name of faith, and where now we share friendship across faiths.

That is a climate change worth celebrating and we recognise the immense role that the Vatican played and continues to play in bringing it about. It was *Nostra Aetate*, 45 years ago, that brought about the single greatest transformation in interfaith relations in recent history, and we recognise your visit here today as a new chapter in that story, and a vital one.

The secularisation of Europe that began in the 17th century did not happen because people lost faith in God. Newton and Descartes, heroes of the Enlightenment, believed in God, very much indeed. What led to secularisation was that

people lost faith in the ability of people of faith to live peaceably together; and we must never go down that road again. We remember the fine words of John Henry Cardinal Newman, who said, 'We should ever conduct ourselves towards our enemy as if he were one day to be our friend,' as well as your own words, in *Caritas in Veritate*, that 'the development of peoples depends... on a recognition that the human race is a single family, working together in true communion, not simply a group of subjects who happen to live side by side.'

We celebrate both our commonalities and differences, because if we had nothing in common we could not communicate, and if we had everything in common, we would have nothing to say. You have spoken of the Catholic Church as a creative minority. And perhaps that is what we should all aspire to be, creative minorities, inspiring one another, and bringing our different gifts to the common good.

Britain has been so enriched by its minorities, by every group represented here today and the intricate harmonies of our several voices and one of our commonalities is that we surely all believe that faith has a major role in strengthening civil society.

In the face of a deeply individualistic culture, we offer community. Against consumerism, we talk about the things that have value but not a price. Against cynicism, we dare to admire and respect. In the face of fragmenting families, we believe in consecrating relationships. We believe in marriage as a commitment, parenthood as a responsibility, and the poetry of everyday life; when it is etched, in homes and schools, with the charisma of holiness and grace.

In our communities, we value people not for what they earn, or what they buy, or how they vote, but for what they are; every one of them a fragment of the Divine Presence. We hold life holy; and each of us is lifted by the knowledge that we are part of something greater than all of us, that created us in forgiveness and love, and asks us to create in forgiveness and love. Each of us in our own way is a guardian of values that are in danger of being lost, in our short-attention span, hyperactive, information-saturated, wisdom-starved age. And though our faiths are profoundly different, yet we recognise in one another the presence of faith itself, that habit of the heart that listens to the music beneath the noise, and knows that God is the point at which soul touches soul and is enlarged by the presence of otherness.

You have honoured us with your presence, and we honour you. May you continue to lead with wisdom and generosity of spirit, and may all our efforts combine to become a blessing to humanity and to God.

The Chief Rabbi, Lord Sacks

Dr Khaled Azzam, Director, The Prince's School of Traditional Arts; Speech delivered to His Holiness Pope Benedict XVI

The Waldegrave Drawing Room, St Mary's, Twickenham 12:40 pm 17 September 2010

Holy Father and Distinguished Guests,

I am honoured to be asked to speak at this auspicious occasion, today, which has gathered such a distinguished audience from many faiths and backgrounds. In the Koran it is said : 'People, We created you all from a single man and a single woman, and made you into nations and tribes so that you may come to know one another.'

The individual divine messages we have received give us the means to realise not only the purpose of our daily existence but also to fulfil our potential as human beings in eternity. These divine messages are therefore interpreted both in terms of a moral code that allows us to interact as fellow human beings in this world; and as a series of metaphysical principles that enable us to transcend our physical state and understand our direct relationship to God.

It is thus that we can live our lives with the full knowledge that the divine touches every aspect of our being. This intervention of the divine in our lives expresses itself through a series of manifestations which follow a clear hierarchical structure. On the first level, which is the level of our physical existence, it places us in an environment and gives us the responsibility for its well being. On the second level it gives us a religious and moral code which binds our communities together and from which civilisations emerge. On the highest level (the level of the Spirit) it allows us the privilege of the consciousness of an absolute reality from which we come and unto which we return.

I am speaking here today amongst believers but it is a fact that we all face a world which has mainly chosen to deny or ignore the divine in our lives — and we are seeing everywhere around us the full consequences of that choice.

As human beings, we have the free will to choose a religious life or not; and to decide whether we believe in the existence of God or not; but what we cannot deny is that we all exist and can never escape from a certain order which I can only describe as the Natural Order – every day we all witness the majesty of the rising and setting sun; we are all moved by the gentle beauty of the moon and we have always structured our lives according to the cycle of the four seasons. This order is what binds all creation together, in a harmonious whole which constantly creates realms of multiplicity from an underlying principle of unity.

And yet, this natural order is often interpreted simply as a cycle of existence which we need to preserve and extend for our physical wellbeing. The focus on ecology and the environment has become a religion of the modern world. Although one can never deny the need to treat the physical world responsibly, we have to realise that this 'religion of ecology' does not fully address the true role of man as vicegerent of God on Earth. It also does not extend the understanding of the cycle of creation into a means of fulfilling our role in eternity.

This limited understanding of our role on Earth is directly connected to the loss of the capacity to understand the language of symbolism - which is one of the fundamental means of expression of the Divine revelation. It is tragic to realise that we have simply lost the ability to understand the language that God speaks to us through his creation – 'We shall show them Our signs in every region of the earth and in themselves until it becomes clear to them that this is the Truth'

The work that we do at the Prince's School of Traditional Arts (established a few years ago now, by His Royal Highness the Prince of Wales) goes some way to regain this understanding of the language of symbolism - which leads to the consciousness of universal principles and not just of historical and geographical facts. One of the main disciplines we teach is the science of geometry which we practise as a means for our students to understand God's creative principle and its manifestation in the order of nature. I can give a brief but moving example of this understanding: we know of no two snowflakes that ever fell to the ground that are the same; yet all snowflakes originate and are held together by the order of six-fold geometry.

I would also like to stress the importance of this discipline of geometry by quoting from the Rasail of Ikhwan elSafa - who were fundamental in the transfer of Platonic thought to the Islamic world in the 11th century:

'Know, oh brother, that the study of sensible geometry leads to skill in all practical arts, while the study of intelligible geometry leads to skill in the intellectual arts because this science is one of the gates through which we move to the knowledge of the essence of the soul and that is the root of knowledge.'

I fully believe that the true understanding of the natural order of being (and its manifestation within us as well as around us) can lead Humankind today to transcend historical and geographical differences as well as individual and sometimes exclusive ownership of the divine - and allow us to fulfil our lives as harmonious elements of the one creative order.

Dr Khaled Azzam delivers his Address

THE ADDRESS OF THE HOLY FATHER

His Holiness Pope Benedict XVI's Address to Representatives of other Religions

The Waldegrave Drawing Room,
St Mary's University College, Twickenham
12:45 pm Friday 17 September

Distinguished guests, dear friends,

I am very pleased to have this opportunity to meet you, the representatives of the various religious communities in Great Britain. I greet both the ministers of religion present and those of you who are active in politics, business and industry. I am grateful to Dr Azzam and to Chief Rabbi Lord Sacks for the greetings which they have expressed on your behalf. As I salute you, let me also wish the Jewish community in Britain and throughout the world a happy and holy celebration of Yom Kippur.

I would like to begin my remarks by expressing the Catholic Church's appreciation for the important witness that all of you bear as spiritual men and women living at a time when religious convictions are not always understood or appreciated. The presence of committed believers in various fields of social and economic life speaks eloquently of the fact that the spiritual dimension of our lives is fundamental to our identity as human beings, that man, in other words, does not live by bread alone (cf. Deut 8:3). As followers of different religious traditions working together for the good of the community at large, we attach great importance to this 'side by side' dimension of our co-operation, which complements the 'face to face' aspect of our continuing dialogue.

On the spiritual level, all of us, in our different ways, are personally engaged in a journey that grants an answer to the most important question of all – the question concerning the ultimate meaning of our human existence. The quest for the sacred is the search for the one thing necessary, which alone satisfies the longings of the human heart. In the 5th century, Saint Augustine described that search in these terms: 'Lord, you have created us for yourself and our hearts are restless until they rest in you' (Confessions, Book I, 1). As we embark on this adventure we come to realise more and more that the initiative lies not with us, but with the Lord: it is not so much we who are seeking him, but rather he who is seeking us, indeed it was he who placed that longing for him deep within our hearts.

Your presence and witness in the world points towards the fundamental importance for human life of this spiritual quest in which we are engaged. Within their own spheres of competence, the human and natural sciences

provide us with an invaluable understanding of aspects of our existence and they deepen our grasp of the workings of the physical universe, which can then be harnessed in order to bring great benefit to the human family. Yet these disciplines do not and cannot answer the fundamental question, because they operate on another level altogether. They cannot satisfy the deepest longings of the human heart, they cannot fully explain to us our origin and our destiny, why and for what purpose we exist, nor indeed can they provide us with an exhaustive answer to the question, 'Why is there something rather than nothing?'

The quest for the sacred does not devalue other fields of human enquiry. On the contrary, it places them in a context which magnifies their importance, as ways of responsibly exercising our stewardship over creation. In the Bible, we read that, after the work of creation was completed, God blessed our first parents and said to them, 'Be fruitful and multiply, and fill the earth and subdue it' (Gen 1:28). He entrusted us with the task of exploring and harnessing the mysteries of nature in order to serve a higher good. What is that higher good? In the Christian faith, it is expressed

as love for God and love for our neighbour. And so we engage with the world wholeheartedly and enthusiastically, but always with a view to serving that higher good, lest we disfigure the beauty of creation by exploiting it for selfish purposes.

So it is that genuine religious belief points us beyond present utility towards the transcendent. It reminds us of the possibility and the imperative of moral conversion, of the duty to live peaceably with our neighbour, of the importance of living a life of integrity. Properly understood, it brings enlightenment, it purifies our hearts and it inspires noble and generous action, to the benefit of the entire human family. It motivates us to cultivate the practice of virtue and to reach out towards one another in love, with the greatest respect for religious traditions different from our own.

Ever since the Second Vatican Council, the Catholic Church has placed special emphasis on the importance of dialogue and co-operation with the followers of other religions. In order to be fruitful, this requires reciprocity on the part of all partners in dialogue and the followers of other religions. I am thinking in particular of situations in some parts of the world, where co-operation

and dialogue between religions calls for mutual respect, the freedom to practise one's religion and to engage in acts of public worship, and the freedom to follow one's conscience without suffering ostracism or persecution, even after conversion from one religion to another. Once such a respect and openness has been established, peoples of all religions will work together effectively for peace and mutual understanding, and so give a convincing witness before the world.

This kind of dialogue needs to take place on a number of different levels, and should not be limited to formal discussions. The dialogue of life involves simply living alongside one another and learning from one another in such a way as to grow in mutual knowledge and respect. The dialogue of action brings us together in concrete forms of collaboration, as we apply our religious insights to the task of promoting integral human development, working for peace, justice and the stewardship of creation. Such a dialogue may include exploring together how to defend human life at every stage and how to ensure the non-exclusion of the religious dimension of individuals

and communities in the life of society. Then at the level of formal conversations, there is a need not only for theological exchange, but also sharing our spiritual riches, speaking of our experience of prayer and contemplation, and expressing to one another the joy of our encounter with divine love. In this context, I am pleased to note the many positive initiatives undertaken in this country to promote such dialogue at a variety of levels. As the Catholic Bishops of England and Wales noted in their recent document '*Meeting God in Friend and Stranger*', the effort to reach out in friendship to followers of other religions is becoming a familiar part of the mission of the local Church (n. 228), a characteristic feature of the religious landscape in this country.

My dear friends, as I conclude my remarks, let me assure you that the Catholic Church follows the path of engagement and dialogue out of a genuine sense of respect for you and your beliefs. Catholics, both in Britain and throughout the world, will continue to work to build bridges of friendship to other religions, to heal past wrongs and to foster trust between individuals and communities. Let me reiterate my thanks for your welcome and my gratitude for this opportunity to offer you my encouragement for your dialogue with your Christian sisters and brothers. Upon all of you I invoke abundant divine blessings! Thank you very much.

Pope Benedict XVI greets Leaders of other Faiths

The quest for the sacred does not devalue other fields of human enquiry. On the contrary, it places them in a context which magnifies their importance, as ways of responsibly exercising our stewardship over creation.

- Pope Benedict XVI

REFLECTIONS

The Right Honourable the Lord Sacks, Chief Rabbi of the United Hebrew Congregations of the Commonwealth

A Reflection on the Papal Visit and on welcoming His Holiness Pope Benedict XVI to the Meeting with Religious Leaders and People of Faith at Twickenham

Welcoming the Pope on behalf of leaders of the non-Christian Faiths in Britain was a moment I will never forget. The Meeting in itself showed the importance to the Vatican, to His Holiness, and to all of us, of respect and friendship between faiths. Too often there has been hostility in place of love, conflict in place of conciliation, and a denial of the holiness of otherness – the very thing we should have learned from the Holiness and Otherness of God.

But there was a deeper resonance to this encounter, given the long, tear-stained history of the Catholic-Jewish relationship. I would like to say what his visit meant to me personally as a Jew.

Over the centuries, the relationship between the Church and the Jews has been one of the saddest stories in the history of religion. The story might have continued were it not for the darkest night of all, the Holocaust. In the wake of that event, a very great Pope indeed, Pope John XXIII, who had helped save many lives in the war years, began to reflect on the history of Christian attitudes toward the Jews, and came to the conclusion that those attitudes must change.

In 1962, he convened the Second Vatican Council, setting in motion what became three years later, though he did not live to see it, the declaration *Nostra Aetate*, 'In Our Age.' It redefined the relationship between the Catholic Church and other faiths, especially Judaism and Islam. It was one of the greatest acts of reconciliation in religious history, and today Catholics and Jews meet not as enemies or strangers, but as friends.

Pope Benedict's London meeting with leaders of many faiths continues that story and widens its embrace. And by one of those coincidences that seem providential, the night of that meeting, this Friday, was the beginning of the holiest day of the Jewish year, the Day of Atonement, our festival of forgiveness.

When I finished my words of welcome, the Pope clasped both my hands, told me how much he valued the Catholic-Jewish relationship, and how much he wanted the work to continue and deepen. It was an epiphany. Soul touched soul across the boundaries of faith, and there was a blessed moment of healing.

Bhai Sahib Bhai Mohinder Singh Chairman, Guru Nanak Nishkam Sewak Jatha (British Sikh Consultative Forum)

A Reflection on the State Visit to the United Kingdom of His Holiness Pope Benedict XVI

As I stood to greet Her Majesty The Queen and Pope Benedict in Edinburgh, I marvelled at the history of the monarchy, and it palaces, pomp and colour. I was particularly grateful, as a Sikh, to have been allowed to carry my Sri Sahib whilst wearing on my body my small Kirpan; this was a significant gesture of respect between one faith and another.

I felt that the Holy Father spoke not only to Catholics but to all the people of the United Kingdom. One could feel powerful vibrations of shared responsibility, unity and hope in his speeches.

The event at St Mary's University College in Twickenham was a celebration of faith and dialogue between religions. One felt the need for enhanced interfaith respect and co-operation and the need to sacrifice one's self for the other.

At the Palace of Westminster, I was thrilled by the Pope's statements on the positive role of religion in public life. I was also reminded of the United Kingdom's family of faiths' 'Shared Act of Reflection and Commitment' made here in 2000 which was reinforced at the launch of the United Kingdom's first Interfaith Week, 2009. To be religious is to be inter-religious (cf. the tenth Sikh Guru, Guru Gobind Singh Ji (1666-1708): 'the whole of humanity is one race').

The spirit of the enormous gathering in Cofton Park was overwhelming; the event was truly electric. The drizzle and rain before the actual commencement was a test of faith for all who had congregated. My first-witnessed Christian Beatification ceremony of an exalted human being, Cardinal John Henry Newman, was poignant, uplifting and inspirational. The importance of perpetuating different faiths and their traditions was re-emphasised.

The Holy Father's visit was a great success; his message was global and relevant to contemporary issues. Condemnation and intolerance cannot drown goodness; love and humility conquer all.

A FRATERNAL VISIT TO THE ARCHBISHOP OF CANTERBURY

The Most Reverend Dr Rowan Williams, Archbishop of Canterbury. An Address to His Holiness Pope Benedict XVI

Lambeth Palace
4:30 pm 17 September 2010

Your Holiness, brother bishops, brothers and sisters in Christ:

It is a particular pleasure that on this historic occasion we are able to come together as bishops of the Roman Catholic and Anglican churches in this country to greet you, Your Holiness, during a visit which we all hope will be of significance both to the Church of Christ and to British society. Your consistent and penetrating analysis of the state of European society in general has been a major contribution to public debate on the relations between Church and culture, and we gratefully acknowledge our debt in this respect.

Our task as bishops is to preach the Gospel and shepherd the flock of Christ; and this includes the responsibility not only to feed the flock, but also to protect it from harm. Today, this involves a readiness to respond to the various trends in our cultural environment that seek to present Christian faith as both an obstacle to human freedom and a scandal to human intellect. We need to be clear that the Gospel of the new creation in Jesus Christ is the door through which we enter into true liberty and true understanding: we are made free to be human as God intends us to be human; we are given the illumination that helps us see one another and all created things in the light of divine love and intelligence. As you said in your Inaugural Mass in 2005, recalling your predecessor's first words as Pope, Christ takes away nothing 'that pertains to human freedom or dignity or to the building of a just society... If we let Christ into our lives, we lose absolutely nothing of what makes life free, beautiful and great. Only in his friendship is the great potential of human existence revealed.' (Inaugural Homily, Rome, 24 April 2005).

The Archbishop of Canterbury welcomes the Pope to Lambeth Palace

Our presence here together as British bishops, today, is a sign of the way in which, in this country, we see our task as one and indivisible. The International Anglican-Roman Catholic Commission on Unity and Mission has set before us all the vital importance of our common calling as bishops, to be agents of mission. Our fervent prayer is that this visit will give us fresh energy and vision for working together in this context in the name of what a great Roman Catholic thinker of the last century called 'true humanism' – a passionate commitment to the dignity of all human beings, from the beginning to the end of life, and to a resistance to every tyranny that threatens to stifle or deny the place of the transcendent in human affairs.

We do not, as churches, seek political power or control, or the dominance of Christian faith in the public sphere; but the opportunity to testify, to argue, sometimes to protest, sometimes to affirm – to play our part in the public debates of our societies. And we shall, of course, be effective not when we have mustered enough political leverage to get our way but when we have persuaded our neighbours that the life of faith is a life well lived and joyfully lived.

In other words, we shall be effective defenders or proclaimers of our faith when we can show what a holy life looks like, a life in which the joy of God is transparently present. And this means that our ministry together as bishops across the still-surviving boundaries of our confessions is not only a search for how we best act together in the public arena; it is a quest together for holiness and transparency to God, a search for ways in which we may help each other to grow in the life of the Holy Spirit. As you have said, Your Holiness, 'a joint fundamental testimony of faith ought to be given before a world which is torn by doubts and shaken by fears.' ('Luther and the Unity of the Churches', 1983)

In 1845, when John Henry Newman finally decided that he must follow his conscience and seek his future in serving God in communion with the See of Rome, one of his most intimate Anglican friends and allies, the priest, Edward Bouverie Pusey, (whose memory the Church of England

marked in its liturgical calendar yesterday) wrote a moving meditation on this 'parting of friends' in which he said of the separation between Anglicans and Roman Catholics: 'it is what is unholy on both sides that keeps us apart'.

That should not surprise us: holiness is, at its simplest, fellowship with Christ; and when that fellowship with Christ is brought to maturity, so is our fellowship with one another. As bishops, we are servants of the unity of Christ's people, Christ's one Body. And, meeting as we do as bishops of separated church communities, we must all feel that each of our own ministries is made less by the fact of our dividedness, a very real but imperfect communion. Perhaps we shall not quickly overcome the remaining obstacles to full, restored communion; but no obstacles stand in the way of our seeking, as a matter of joyful obedience to the Lord, more ways in which to build up one another in holiness by prayer and public celebration together, by closer friendship, and by growing together both in the challenging work of service for all whom Christ loves, and mission to all God has made.

May this historic visit be for all of us a special time of grace and of growth in our shared calling, as you, Your Holiness, bring us the word of the Gospel afresh.

THE ADDRESS OF THE HOLY FATHER

His Holiness Pope Benedict XVI's Address to the Archbishop of Canterbury

Lambeth Palace
4:40 pm Friday 17 September 2010

Your Grace,

It is a pleasure for me to be able to return the courtesy of the visits you have made to me in Rome by a fraternal visit to you here in your official residence. I thank you for your invitation and for the hospitality that you have so generously provided. I greet too the Anglican Bishops gathered here from different parts of the United Kingdom, my brother Bishops from the Catholic Dioceses of England, Wales and Scotland, and the ecumenical advisers who are present.

You have spoken, Your Grace, of the historic meeting that took place, almost thirty years ago, between two of our predecessors – Pope John Paul the Second and Archbishop Robert Runcie – in Canterbury Cathedral. There, in the very place where Saint Thomas of Canterbury bore witness to Christ by the shedding of his blood, they prayed together for the gift of unity among the followers of Christ. We continue today to pray for that gift, knowing that the unity Christ willed for his disciples will only come about in answer to prayer, through the action of the Holy Spirit, who ceaselessly renews the Church and guides her into the fullness of truth.

It is not my intention today to speak of the difficulties that the ecumenical path has encountered and continues to encounter. Those difficulties are well known to everyone here. Rather, I wish to join you in giving thanks for the deep friendship that has grown between us and for the remarkable progress that has been made in so many areas of dialogue during the forty years that have elapsed since the Anglican-Roman Catholic International Commission began its work. Let us entrust the fruits of that work to the Lord of the harvest, confident that he will bless our friendship with further significant growth.

The context in which dialogue takes place between the Anglican Communion and the Catholic Church has evolved in dramatic ways since the private meeting between Pope John XXIII and Archbishop Geoffrey Fisher in 1960. On the one hand, the surrounding culture is growing ever more distant from its Christian roots, despite a deep and widespread hunger for spiritual nourishment. On the other hand, the increasingly multicultural dimension of society, particularly marked in this country, brings with it the opportunity to encounter other religions. For us Christians this opens up the possibility of exploring, together with members of other religious traditions, ways of bearing witness to the transcendent dimension of the human person and the universal call to holiness, leading to the practice of virtue in our personal and social lives. Ecumenical co-operation in this task remains essential, and will surely bear fruit in promoting peace and harmony in a world that so often seems at risk of fragmentation.

At the same time, we Christians must never hesitate to proclaim our faith in the uniqueness of the salvation won for us by Christ, and to explore together a deeper understanding of the means he has placed at our disposal for attaining that salvation. God 'wants all to be saved, and to come to the knowledge of the truth' (1 Tim 2:4), and that truth is nothing other than Jesus Christ, eternal Son of the Father, who has reconciled all things in himself by the power of his Cross. In fidelity to the Lord's will, as expressed in that passage from Saint Paul's First Letter to Timothy, we recognise that the Church is called to be inclusive, yet never at the expense of Christian truth. Herein lies the dilemma facing all who are genuinely committed to the ecumenical journey.

In the figure of John Henry Newman, who is to be beatified on Sunday, we celebrate a churchman whose ecclesial vision was nurtured by his Anglican background and matured during his many years of ordained ministry in the Church of England. He can teach us the virtues that ecumenism demands: on the one hand, he was moved to follow his conscience, even at great personal cost; and on the other hand, the warmth of his continued friendship with his former colleagues, led him to explore with them, in a truly eirenical spirit, the questions on which they differed, driven by a deep longing for unity in faith. Your Grace, in that same spirit of friendship, let us renew our determination to pursue the goal of unity in faith, hope, and love, in accordance with the will of our one Lord and Saviour Jesus Christ.

With these sentiments, I take my leave of you. 'May the grace of the Lord Jesus Christ and the love of God and the fellowship of the Holy Spirit be with you all' (2 Cor 13:13).

A REFLECTION

The Right Reverend Stephen Platten, Bishop of Wakefield

A Reflection on the Fraternal Visit to the Archbishop of Canterbury in Lambeth Palace, written as former Co-Secretary of ARCIC II

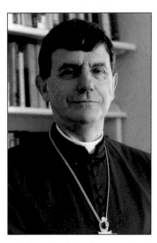

Lambeth Palace is a setting of great resonance for the meeting of fifty or more bishops from the Church of England, the Church in Wales and the Roman Catholic Church in England and Wales. Lambeth has been the London residence of the Archbishops of Canterbury for more than eight hundred years; four hundred of these years preceded the Reformation in the then-united Church of the West.

This was the first visit of a Pope to Lambeth Palace, and history, theology and worship were all themes that came together in what were sacred moments. We were united in prayer and in our appreciation of the addresses from both the Archbishop of Canterbury and the Holy Father.

Pope Benedict gave thanks for our friendship and the unity in the Gospel we already share. He said that he did not wish to focus on the things that still divide us. Rather, he wanted to give thanks for the extraordinary progress that has been made through God's grace.

The Holy Father looked back on the remarkable journey of the past forty years, notably through the work of ARCIC, the Anglican-Roman Catholic International Commission. Let us celebrate these fruits, he said, and let them be harvested by Christ, the Lord of the harvest.

The Archbishop had alluded in his address to Edward Bouverie Pusey's words on John Henry Newman's submission to the Holy See in 1845.

Pusey had reflected that it is only unholinesses that still divide us. The Archbishop reflected that it is still so. The Holy Father also referred to Newman and saw in him signs of the ecumenical spirit; conscience should always be a primary concern, but friendship binds all.

The meeting was enormously encouraging to me as I had previously lived almost six years of my life at Lambeth Palace, and during that time was the Anglican co-secretary of ARCIC II.

Evening Prayer in Westminster Abbey crowned the day. There is unquestionably more hope along the path to unity between our two Churches. If there has been an ecumenical winter, then be prepared for the beginning of the thaw.

The Right Reverend Christopher Hill, Bishop of Guildford

A Reflection on the Meeting of Anglican and Roman Catholic Diocesan Bishops at Lambeth Palace and on attending Evening Prayer at Westminster Abbey, in his role as former Anglican Co-Secretary of ARCIC I and being in the senior Anglican delegation, under the Archbishop of Canterbury, welcoming His Holiness Pope Benedict XVI

I first met Pope Benedict, as Cardinal Joseph Ratzinger, in a long but cordial discussion about the work of the Anglican-Roman Catholic International Commission.

On the Pope's arrival at Lambeth Palace, the

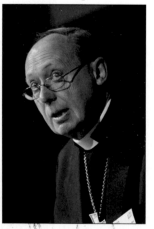

Holy Father and the Archbishop of Canterbury warmly embraced each other and introductions were then made. In the Great Hall of Lambeth Palace, the Pope and Primate met in the significant presence of the two episcopates, Anglican and Roman Catholic. That was the special thing about the

Lambeth meeting. Since the visit of Pope John Paul II, deep friendships and trust have developed; as the two episcopates regularly meet together. Before the Pope arrived at Lambeth Palace, Anglican and Roman Catholic bishops mingled as genuine friends.

The Lambeth message was: 'in spite of the problems we should do much more together on the ground'. This should give impetus to the aspiration of the International Anglican Roman Catholic Commission for Unity in Mission, established some years ago to complement the theological discussions.

In Westminster Hall, Pope Benedict's stress on the need for a serious dialogue between faith and reason, and the need for an ethical basis for political policy, was profoundly welcome.

In Westminster Abbey, Pope Benedict and the Archbishop of Canterbury presided jointly over an ecumenical Evening Prayer in the church of the Queen and the nation, dedicated to Saint Peter, and amid conscious memories of the Benedictine community which went before.

The Archbishop spoke of Saint Benedict to Pope Benedict, and of Pope Saint Gregory the Great who sent Saint Augustine to Canterbury, bearing witness to the Gospel. An ancient text of the Gospels actually brought from Rome by Augustine was movingly venerated by the Pope and Archbishop.

The message was clear: the worship of God the Holy Trinity comes before all things; and what we have in common in Christ, is more significant than that which divides.

Commissioner Elizabeth Matear, Territorial Leader of the Salvation Army in the United Kingdom

A Reflection on Evening Prayer in Westminster Abbey made as Moderator of the Free Churches Group and Co-President of Churches Together in England

The visit of His Holiness Pope Benedict XVI to the United Kingdom has been a most significant event. As a church leader and a privileged representative of the Free Churches in England and

Wales, I have a deep awareness of history and the common heritage that we share. As we gathered together in Westminster Abbey, the place of our nation's joy and tears in so many ways, we walked together and sat together in friendship and Christian love. I reflected that in just a few hours the journey of His Holiness had taken him to some of the iconic places of our country's history.

As a Scot, I followed with interest the journey to Holyrood House and recalled the past events that shaped our nation. Here in London, the visits to Lambeth Palace, the Palace of Westminster and Westminster Abbey, had huge historical significance and heavy symbolism.

The day's reflections for me were not just of the past, but of the present and the future. We lean on the past, we are shaped by the past, but we cannot live in the past. The Gospel of Jesus Christ is always relevant and contemporary. In my heart, I felt that the presence of Pope Benedict XVI in the United Kingdom spoke volumes. For our Catholic brothers and sisters it brought faith, encouragement and challenge. Together as the Body of Christ, we heard a voice to challenge the role of faith in our society, beyond the historical or symbolic, to the place of reality and relevance.

We gathered together, conscious of collective failings and weakness, but joined by the Holy Spirit we met in unity and humility, under the banner of Love. This was a moment of history and I was so glad to be part of it.

We Christians must never hesitate to proclaim our faith in the uniqueness of the salvation won for us by Christ... - Pope Benedict XVI

ADDRESS TO CIVIL SOCIETY IN WESTMINSTER HALL

The Pope enters Westminster Hall and history

The History of Westminster Hall

Almost one thousand years of the Nation's history are contained within the ancient walls of Westminster Hall at the Palace of Westminster. Westminster Hall, which was built in the 11th century and was once the largest hall in Europe, has served numerous functions down the centuries.

From the 12th century onwards, following the service in Westminster Abbey, the Hall was also used for the coronation banquets of every monarch from King Richard I (1189) until King George IV (1821).

Westminster Hall was gradually appropriated by the judiciary, with the first judges sitting there by 1178. It was the place in which the English legal system was developed over several centuries. The Royal Courts of Justice sat here until 1882, when they were removed to the Strand.

The Hall witnessed many great state trials, examples from the 16th, 17th and 18th centuries including those of Saint Philip Howard, (20th) Earl of Arundel, King Charles I and George Seton, (5th) Earl of Winton and Catholic martyrs Sir Thomas More and Edmund Campion, who were tried for treason, subsequently found guilty and ordered to be executed. Thomas More was canonised by Pope Pius XI in 1935, the 400th anniversary of his death. For Catholics, it is a place made sacred by the blood of the many martyrs who were condemned within its walls.

The Hall has been used for the Lying in State of monarchs and queen consorts, since King Edward VII; and of two great statesmen, William Ewart Gladstone and Sir Winston Churchill. Most recently in 2002, Her Majesty Queen Elizabeth the Queen Mother lay in State in Westminster Hall.

Address given by the Speaker of the House of Commons, The Right Honourable John Bercow to His Holiness Pope Benedict XVI

Westminster Hall, City of Westminster
5:30 pm Friday 17 September 2010

It is my honour to introduce His Holiness Pope Benedict XVI to Westminster Hall and, through this fine edifice, to the Palace of Westminster as a whole. It is the first time that a Pontiff has visited the Hall, a fact that alone invests today with deep historical significance. It is a measure of the distance we have come and the dialogue which we have created over the past few decades that an event which in years gone by, would have been thought inconceivable can occur and seem wholly natural.

This Hall is the oldest structure of its kind in Europe and the repository of many memories. It is, inevitably, associated with trials and condemnation to death – as was the fate of Sir Thomas More, one of my 156 predecessors as Speaker of the House of Commons, and of King Charles I, since considered a martyr by many Anglicans. Yet it would be a mistake to think of Westminster Hall only in these

The distinguished audience in Westminster Hall applauds Pope Benedict

terms, when it has been as much a stage for robust debate as for sheer intolerance.

That tradition of debate has roots far deeper than those of contemporary democracy. It was here in 1374, for example, that a notable discussion occurred between three religious thinkers – a Franciscan, a Dominican and a Benedictine – on the precise relationship between the Papacy and the temporal affairs of their kingdom. Suffice to say that no consensus was reached on that occasion. Nevertheless, it is the right to ask such questions, and to deliberate the merits of alternative answers, that makes for freedom. Naturally, Parliament contains Members with a wide range of views on great ethical issues. However, as is well known, the House of Commons and the House of Lords, over decades, have taken positions on social, scientific, and sexual issues which are different from those of the Vatican. It is surely right to have robust but respectful debate on such issues within Parliament, between our institutions, and throughout civil society. A very difficult past, and a turbulent present, need not be a barrier to an enlightened future.

History means that those of us privileged to serve society as its elected representatives arrive in this Palace of Westminster, to be immediately reminded of the relationship between Church and State. We are conscious of a healthy tension in this relationship as we seek to do our business. Your presence, Most Holy Father, adds to the rich tapestry of the past and provides further reason for the many hundreds of thousands of people who come here every year to contemplate the character of this building and what has been witnessed in it. Faith is not a relic either in political discourse or in modern society but is embedded in its fabric.

The warmth of the greeting extended by Her Majesty The Queen yesterday to the Holy Father was notable. Today, in this Hall, (which sits at the heart of our democratic tradition), are gathered many elected Members of Parliament, Members of the House of Lords, and numerous other distinguished guests from all walks of life and all parts of the United Kingdom. On behalf of everyone here, I warmly welcome you and invite you to address us.

Pope Benedict XVI meets former Prime Ministers, the Deputy Prime Minister and other distinguished guests

ADDRESS OF THE HOLY FATHER IN WESTMINSTER HALL

His Holiness Pope Benedict XVI's Address to Politicians, Diplomats, Academics and Business Leaders

Westminster Hall, City of Westminster
5:40 pm Friday 17 September 2010

Mr Speaker,

Thank you for your words of welcome on behalf of this distinguished gathering. As I address you, I am conscious of the privilege afforded me to speak to the British people and their representatives in Westminster Hall, a building of unique significance in the civil and political history of the people of these islands. Allow me also to express my esteem for the Parliament which has existed on this site for centuries and which has had such a profound influence on the development of participative government among the nations, especially in the Commonwealth and the English-speaking world at large. Your common law tradition serves as the basis of legal systems in many parts of the world, and your particular vision of the respective rights and duties of the state and the individual, and of the separation of powers, remains an inspiration to many across the globe.

As I speak to you in this historic setting, I think of the countless men and women down the centuries who have played their part in the momentous events that have taken place within these walls and have shaped the lives of many generations of Britons, and others besides. In particular, I recall the figure of Saint Thomas More, the great English scholar and statesman, who is admired by believers and non-believers alike for the integrity with which he followed his conscience, even at the cost of displeasing the Sovereign whose 'good servant'

he was, because he chose to serve God first. The dilemma which faced More in those difficult times, the perennial question of the relationship between what is owed to Caesar and what is owed to God, allows me the opportunity to reflect with you briefly on the proper place of religious belief within the political process.

This country's parliamentary tradition owes much to the national instinct for moderation, to the desire to achieve a genuine balance between the legitimate claims of government and the rights of those subject to it. While decisive steps have been taken at several points in your history to place limits on the exercise of power, the nation's political institutions have been able to evolve with a remarkable degree of stability. In the process, Britain has emerged as a pluralist democracy which places great value on freedom of speech, freedom of political affiliation and respect for the rule of law, with a strong sense of the individual's rights and duties, and of the equality of all citizens before the law. While couched in different language, Catholic social teaching has much in common with this approach, in its over-riding concern to safeguard the unique dignity of every human person, created in the image and likeness of God,

and in its emphasis on the duty of civil authority to foster the common good.

And yet the fundamental questions at stake in Thomas More's trial continue to present themselves in ever-changing terms as new social conditions emerge. Each generation, as it seeks to advance the common good, must ask anew: what are the requirements that governments may reasonably impose upon citizens, and how far do they extend? By appeal to what authority can moral dilemmas be resolved? These questions take us directly to the ethical foundations of civil discourse. If the moral principles underpinning the democratic process are themselves determined by nothing more solid than social consensus, then the fragility of the process becomes all too evident - herein lies the real challenge for democracy.

The inadequacy of pragmatic, short-term solutions to complex social and ethical problems has been illustrated all too clearly by the recent global financial crisis. There is widespread agreement that the lack of a solid ethical foundation for economic activity has contributed to the grave difficulties now being experienced by millions of people throughout the world. Just as 'every economic decision has a moral consequence' (*Caritas in*

Veritate, 37), so too in the political field, the ethical dimension of policy has far-reaching consequences that no government can afford to ignore. A positive illustration of this is found in one of the British Parliament's particularly notable achievements – the abolition of the slave trade. The campaign that led to this landmark legislation was built upon firm ethical principles, rooted in the natural law, and it has made a contribution to civilisation of which this nation may be justly proud.

The central question at issue, then, is this: where is the ethical foundation for political choices to be found? The Catholic tradition maintains that the objective norms governing right action are accessible to reason, prescinding from the content of revelation. According to this understanding, the role of religion in political debate is not so much to supply these norms, as if they could not be known by non-believers – still less to propose concrete political solutions, which would lie altogether outside the competence of religion – but rather to help purify and shed light upon the application of reason to the discovery of objective moral principles. This 'corrective' role of religion *vis-à-vis* reason is not always welcomed, though, partly because distorted forms of religion, such as

sectarianism and fundamentalism, can be seen to create serious social problems themselves. And in their turn, these distortions of religion arise when insufficient attention is given to the purifying and structuring role of reason within religion. It is a two-way process. Without the corrective supplied by religion, though, reason too can fall prey to distortions, as when it is manipulated by ideology, or applied in a partial way that fails to take full account of the dignity of the human person. Such misuse of reason, after all, was what gave rise to the slave trade in the first place and to many other social evils, not least the totalitarian ideologies of the 20th century. This is why I would suggest that the world of reason and the world of faith – the world of secular rationality and the world of religious belief – need one another and should not be afraid to enter into a profound and ongoing dialogue, for the good of our civilisation.

Religion, in other words, is not a problem for legislators to solve, but a vital contributor to the national conversation. In this light, I cannot but voice my concern at the increasing marginalisation of religion, particularly of Christianity, that is taking place in some quarters, even in nations which place a great emphasis on tolerance. There are those who would advocate that the voice of religion be silenced, or at least relegated to the purely private sphere. There are those who argue that the public celebration of festivals such as Christmas should be discouraged, in the questionable belief that it might somehow offend those of other religions or none. And there are those who argue – paradoxically with the intention of eliminating discrimination – that Christians in public roles should be required at times to act against their conscience. These are worrying signs of a failure to appreciate not only the rights of believers to freedom of conscience and freedom of religion, but also the legitimate role of religion in the public square. I would invite all of you, therefore, within your respective spheres of influence, to seek ways of promoting and encouraging dialogue between faith and reason at every level of national life.

Your readiness to do so is already implied in the unprecedented invitation extended to me today. And it finds expression in the fields of concern in which your Government has been engaged with the Holy See. In the area of peace, there have been exchanges regarding the elaboration of an international arms trade treaty; regarding human rights, the Holy See and the United Kingdom have welcomed the spread of democracy, especially in the last 65 years; in the field of development, there has been collaboration on debt relief, fair trade and financing for development, particularly through the International Finance Facility, the International Immunisation Bond, and the Advanced Market Commitment. The Holy See also looks forward to exploring with the United Kingdom new ways to promote environmental responsibility, to the benefit of all.

I also note that the present Government has committed the United Kingdom to devoting 0.7 per cent of national income to development aid by 2013. In recent years it has been encouraging to witness the positive signs of a world-wide growth in solidarity towards the poor. But to turn this solidarity into effective action, calls for fresh thinking that will improve life conditions in many important areas, such as food production, clean water, job creation, education, support to families, (especially migrants), and basic healthcare. Where human lives are concerned, time is always short: yet the world has witnessed the vast resources that governments can draw upon to rescue financial institutions deemed 'too big to fail'. Surely the integral human development of the world's peoples is no less important: here is an enterprise, worthy of the world's attention, that is truly 'too big to fail'.

This overview of recent co-operation between the United Kingdom and the Holy See illustrates well how much progress has been made, in the years that have passed since the establishment of bilateral diplomatic relations, in promoting throughout the world the many core values that we share. I hope and pray that this relationship will continue to bear fruit, and that it will be mirrored in a growing acceptance of the need for dialogue and respect at every level of society between the world of reason and the world of faith. I am convinced that, within this country too, there are many areas in which the Church and the public authorities can work together for the good of citizens, in harmony with this Parliament's historic practice of invoking the Spirit's guidance upon those who seek to improve the conditions of all mankind. For such co-operation to be possible, religious bodies – including institutions linked to the Catholic Church – need to be free to act in accordance with their own principles and specific convictions based upon the faith and the official teaching of the Church. In this way, such basic rights as religious freedom, freedom of conscience and freedom of association are guaranteed. The angels looking down on us from the magnificent ceiling of this ancient hall remind us of the long tradition from which British Parliamentary democracy has evolved. They remind us that God is constantly watching over us to guide and protect us. And they summon us to acknowledge the vital contribution that religious belief has made and can continue to make to the life of the nation.

Mr Speaker, I thank you once again for this opportunity briefly to address this distinguished audience. Let me assure you and the Lord Speaker of my continued good wishes and prayers for you and for the fruitful work of both Houses of this ancient Parliament. Thank you and God bless you all!

The Lord Speaker
The Right Honourable Baroness Hayman

In the Valedictory Address thanking Pope Benedict XVI following his speech, the Lord Speaker, Baroness Hayman, spoke of the contribution in the House of Lords by many religious voices, that includes not only Bishops of the Church of England, but also Muslims and Jews, Hindus and Sikhs and many distinguished Catholic peers. Respecting these voices is essential to Parliament, she said.

The world of reason and the world of faith – the world of secular rationality and the world of religious belief – need one another and should not be afraid to enter into a profound and ongoing dialogue, for the good of our civilisation.

- Pope Benedict XVI

A REFLECTION

The Right Honourable Professor the Lord Alton of Liverpool

A Reflection on the Holy Father's Address to Civil Society in Westminster Hall

If the walls of Westminster Hall could speak, they could tell you most things that you need to know about the history of England.

The sham trials and trumped-up charges of treason levelled against Edmund Campion and Thomas More; the State's determination to force men to choose between their conscience and submission; and the systematic abuse of power and falsified evidence are all parts of the story of the Hall.

I walked through the Hall in 1979 as a young Member of Parliament and I have now worked in the precincts of the Hall for more than 30 years. Westminster Hall is at the very heart of Britain's parliamentary democracy and it was here that former Prime Ministers, political and civic leaders, gathered to hear Pope Benedict XVI remind us that religion still has a vital role to play within our culture.

As we waited for the Pope's arrival, there was a deep appreciation that history was being made, and also that it was being healed.

The Holy Father began his Address by recalling the many men and women who had played their part. In particular he spoke of Saint Thomas More who faced the 'perennial question of the relationship between what is owed to Caesar and what is owed to God'.

It is not enough to live by social consensus - or opinion polls. Religious faith, the Pope said, helps to purify and shed light on the ethics which should underpin political decisions.

I wondered what legislators who had legalised the creation of animal-human hybrid embryos; the abortion of disabled babies up to and even during birth; had imposed party policy on previous conscience questions, such as abortion; or who had supported measures which penalise the poorest members of society, made of this call to place human dignity at the heart of the political equation.

In listening to this thoughtful and challenging address, I also wondered what Campion and More, from their elevated positions, would have made of the day's events. In their final agonies I doubt that either would have foreseen a day when the successor of Peter would be respectfully welcomed at Westminster; but both would surely rejoice.

THE VISIT TO WESTMINSTER ABBEY

The History of Westminster Abbey

*W*estminster Abbey is steeped in more than a thousand years of British history. Benedictine monks first settled on the site in the middle of the 10th century, establishing a tradition of Christian community life that continues to this day.

The Abbey has been the setting for the coronation of our monarchs since 1066, and it is the final resting place of seventeen of them.

The present church, begun in 1245, is one of the most important Gothic buildings in the country; with the shrine of the medieval saint, Edward the Confessor, at its heart. A treasure-house of centuries of art, it has become the place where some of the most significant people and events in the nation's history are remembered.

Its mission, overseen by the Dean and Chapter, is to serve God by offering daily and public worship; to serve the Sovereign by daily prayer and by a ready response to requests; to serve the nation by fostering true religion within national life, maintaining a close relationship with Parliament; and to serve as a place of welcome and prayer for millions of worshippers and visitors.

The Pope shared goodwill and prayers with Christians from across the United Kingdom and from a wide variety of denominations when he took part in the service of Evening Prayer.

Catholic and Protestant banners vie for attention outside Westminster Abbey

The newly crowned Queen Elizabeth II makes her progress up the centre aisle of Westminster Abbey on 2 June 1953

A CELEBRATION OF EVENING PRAYER IN WESTMINSTER ABBEY

The Introductory Words of His Holiness Pope Benedict XVI made during Evening Prayer

Westminster Abbey
Friday 17 September 2010

Your Grace, Mr Dean,
Dear Friends in Christ,

I thank you for your gracious welcome. This noble edifice evokes England's long history, so deeply marked by the preaching of the Gospel and the Christian culture to which it gave birth. I come here today as a pilgrim from Rome, to pray before the tomb of Saint Edward the Confessor and to join you in imploring the gift of Christian unity. May these moments of prayer and friendship confirm us in love for Jesus Christ, our Lord and Saviour, and in common witness to the enduring power of the Gospel to illumine the future of this great nation.

The Address of His Holiness Pope Benedict XVI given at the Conclusion of Evening Prayer

Dear friends in Christ,

I thank the Lord for this opportunity to join you, the representatives of the Christian confessions present in Great Britain, in this magnificent Abbey Church dedicated to Saint Peter, whose architecture and history speak so eloquently of our common heritage of faith. Here we cannot help but be reminded of how greatly the Christian faith shaped the unity and culture of Europe and the heart and spirit of the English people. Here too, we are forcibly reminded that what we share, in Christ, is greater than what continues to divide us.

I am grateful to His Grace the Archbishop of Canterbury for his kind greeting, and to the Dean and Chapter of this venerable Abbey for their cordial welcome. I thank the Lord for allowing me, as the Successor of Saint Peter in the See of Rome, to make this pilgrimage to the tomb of Saint Edward the Confessor. Edward, King of England, remains a model of Christian witness and an example of that true grandeur to which the Lord summons his disciples in the Scriptures we have just heard: the grandeur of a humility and obedience grounded in Christ's own example (cf. Phil 2:6-8), the grandeur of a fidelity which does not hesitate to embrace the mystery of the Cross out of undying love for the divine Master and unfailing hope in his promises (cf. Mk 10:43-44).

This year, as we know, marks the hundredth anniversary of the modern ecumenical movement, which began with the Edinburgh Conference's appeal for Christian unity as the prerequisite for a credible and convincing witness to the Gospel in our time. In commemorating this anniversary, we must give thanks for the remarkable progress made towards this noble goal through the efforts of committed Christians of every denomination. At the same time, however, we remain conscious of how much yet remains to be done. In a world marked by growing interdependence and solidarity, we are challenged to proclaim with renewed conviction the reality of our reconciliation and liberation in Christ, and to propose the truth of the Gospel as the key to an authentic and integral human development. In a society which has become increasingly indifferent or even hostile to the Christian message, we are all the more compelled to give a joyful and convincing account of the hope that is within us (cf. 1 Pet 3:15), and to present the Risen Lord as the response to the deepest questions and spiritual aspirations of the men and women of our time.

As we processed to the chancel at the beginning of this service, the choir sang that Christ is our 'sure foundation'. He is the Eternal Son of God, of one substance with the Father, who took flesh, as the Creed states, 'for us men and for our salvation'. He alone has the words of everlasting life. In him, as the Apostle teaches, 'all things hold together' ... 'for in him all the fullness of God was pleased to dwell' (Col 1:17,19).

Our commitment to Christian unity is born of nothing less than our faith in Christ, in this Christ, risen from the dead and seated at the right hand of the Father, who will come again in glory to judge the living and the dead. It is the reality of Christ's person, his saving work and above all the historical fact of his resurrection, which is the content of the apostolic *kerygma* and those credal formulas which, beginning in the New Testament itself, have guaranteed the integrity of its transmission. The Church's unity, in a word, can never be other than a unity in the apostolic faith, in the faith entrusted to each new member of the Body of Christ during the rite of Baptism. It is this faith which unites us to the Lord, makes us sharers in his Holy Spirit, and thus, even now, sharers in the life of the Blessed Trinity, the model of the Church's *koinonia* here below.

Dear friends, we are all aware of the challenges, the blessings, the disappointments and the signs of hope which have marked our ecumenical journey. Tonight, we entrust all of these to the Lord, confident in his providence and the power of his grace. We know that the friendships we have forged, the dialogue which we have begun and the hope which guides us will provide strength and direction as we persevere on our common journey. At the same time, with evangelical realism, we must also recognise the challenges which confront us, not only along the path of Christian unity, but also in our task of proclaiming Christ in our day. Fidelity to the word of God, precisely because it is a true word, demands of us an obedience which leads us together to a deeper understanding of the Lord's will, an obedience which must be free of intellectual conformism or facile accommodation to the spirit of the age. This is the word of encouragement, which I wish to leave with you this evening, and I do so in fidelity to my ministry as the Bishop of Rome and the Successor of Saint Peter, charged with a particular care for the unity of Christ's flock.

Gathered in this ancient monastic church, we can recall the example of a great Englishman and churchman whom we honour in common: Saint Bede the Venerable. At the dawn of a new age in the life of society and of the Church, Bede understood both the importance of fidelity to the word of God as transmitted by the apostolic tradition, and the need for creative openness to new developments and to the demands of a sound implantation of the Gospel, in contemporary language and culture.

This nation, and the Europe which Bede and his contemporaries helped to build, once again stands at the threshold of a new age. May Saint Bede's example inspire the Christians of these lands to rediscover their shared legacy, to strengthen what they have in common, and to continue their efforts to grow in friendship. May the Risen Lord strengthen our efforts to mend the ruptures of the past and to meet the challenges of the present with hope in the future which, in his providence, he holds out to us and to our world. Amen.

Pope Benedict flanked by the Dean of Westminster and Archbishop Rowan Williams

The Dean explains the Grave of the Unknown Warrior to His Holiness

The Grave of the Unknown Warrior

*A*ll Heads of State on governmental visits are invited to come and lay a wreath at the Grave of the Unknown Warrior, near to the great west door of the Abbey. As Head of the Vatican State, Pope Benedict came to pay his respects at the beginning of Evening Prayer, by saying a prayer for peace at the Grave.

Lord God, you hold both heaven and earth in a single peace. Let the design of your great love shine on the waste of our anger and sorrow, and give peace to your Church, peace among nations, peace in our homes, and peace in our hearts, in Jesus Christ our Lord. Amen.

The Most Reverend Dr Rowan Williams, Archbishop of Canterbury
The Address at Evening Prayer

Westminster Abbey
7:30 pm Friday 17 September 2010

Your Holiness, Members of the Collegiate Body, distinguished guests, brothers and sisters in Christ:

Christians in Britain, especially in England, look back with the most fervent gratitude to the events of 597, when Augustine landed on these shores to preach the gospel to the Anglo-Saxons at the behest of Pope Saint Gregory the Great. For Christians of all traditions and confessions, Saint Gregory is a figure of compelling attractiveness and spiritual authority – pastor and leader, scholar, exegete and spiritual guide. The fact that the first preaching of the Gospel to the English peoples in the 6th and 7th centuries has its origins in his vision, creates a special connection for us with the See of the Apostles Peter and Paul; and Gregory's witness and legacy remain an immensely fruitful source of inspiration for our own mission, in these dramatically different times. Two dimensions of that vision may be of special importance as we reflect today on the significance of Your Holiness's visit to us.

Saint Gregory was the first to spell out for the faithful something of the magnitude of the gift given to Christ's Church through the life of Saint Benedict – to whom you, Your Holiness, have signalled your devotion in the choice of your name as Pope. In Saint Gregory's Dialogues, we can trace the impact of Saint Benedict – an extraordinary man who, through a relatively brief 'Rule of Life', opened up for the whole civilisation of Europe since the 6th century the possibility of living in joy and mutual service, in simplicity and self-denial, in a balanced pattern of labour and prayer in which every moment spoke of human dignity fully realised in surrender to a loving God. The Benedictine Life proved a sure foundation, not only for generations of monks and nuns, but for an entire culture in which productive work and contemplative silence and receptivity - human dignity and human freedom - were both honoured.

Our own culture, a culture in which so often it seems that 'love has grown cold', is one in which we can see the dehumanising effects of losing sight of Benedict's vision. Work is so often an anxious and obsessive matter, as if our whole value as human beings depended upon it; and so, consequently, unemployment, still a scourge and a threat in these uncertain financial times, comes

The Archbishop replies to the Pope, invoking Saints Peter, Paul, (Pope) Gregory and Benedict

to seem like a loss of dignity and meaning in life. We live in an age where there is a desperate need to recover the sense of the dignity of both labour and leisure and the necessity of a silent openness to God that allows our true character to grow and flourish by participating in an eternal love.

In a series of profound and eloquent encyclicals, you have explored these themes for our day, grounding everything in the eternal love of the Holy Trinity, challenging us to hope both for this world and the next, and analysing the ways in which our economic habits have trapped us in a reductive and unworthy style of human living. In this building with its long Benedictine legacy, we acknowledge with gratitude your contribution to a Benedictine vision for our days, and pray that your time with us in Britain may help us all towards a renewal of the hope and energy we need as Christians to witness to our conviction, that in their relation to God men and women may grow into the fullest freedom and beauty of spirit.

And in this, we are recalled also to the importance among the titles of the Bishops of Rome of Pope Saint Gregory's own self-designation as 'servant of the servants of God' — surely the one title that points most directly to the example of the Lord who has called us. There is, we know, no authority in the Church that is not the authority of service: that is, of building up the people of God to full maturity. Christ's service is simply the way in which we meet his almighty power: the power to remake the world he has created, pouring out into our lives, individually and together, what we truly need in order to become fully what we are made to be – the image of the divine life. It is that image which the Pastor in the Church seeks to serve, bowing down in reverence before each human person in the knowledge of the glory for which he or she was made.

Christians have very diverse views about the nature of the vocation that belongs to the See of Rome. Yet, as Your Holiness's great predecessor reminded us all, in his encyclical *Ut Unum Sint*, we must learn to reflect together on how the historic ministry of the Roman Church and its Chief Pastor may speak to the Church catholic - East and West, global north and global south - of the authority of Christ and his apostles to build up the Body in love; how it may be realised as a ministry of patience

Saint Edward the Confessor
King of England (1042-1066)

*W*estminster Abbey is also the shrine of Saint Edward the Confessor. King Edward was declared a saint in 1161 and, two years later, the first shrine was erected. The present shrine, close to the high altar, was part of King Henry III's rebuilt church and was a place of pilgrimage for thousands of people during the Middle Ages, the forerunners of today's tourists.

The Archbishop of Canterbury and Pope Benedict XVI joined in with this long tradition of pilgrims, when they knelt to pray together at the end of the service in the chapel containing the shrine of Saint Edward.

The Archbishop said a Prayer for the Church and the Nations. The Pope said a Prayer for the Unity of the Church.

and reverence towards all, a ministry of creative love and self-giving that leads us all into the same path of seeking not our own comfort or profit, but the good of the entire human community and the glory of God the Creator and Redeemer.

We pray that your time with us will be a further step for all of us into the mystery of the cross and the resurrection, so that growing together we may become more effective channels for God's purpose to heal the wounds of humankind, and to restore once again both in our societies and our environment the likeness of his glory as revealed in the face of Jesus Christ.

Queen Catherine de Valois

Pope Benedict prayed at the Tomb of Saint Edward the Confessor, with the Archbishop of Canterbury, near to the Chapel of King Henry V, where the tomb, therein, of Queen Catherine de Valois, linked Her Majesty's mother, Princess Isabelle of Bavaria, to the Pope's own Bavarian background. Queen Catherine was the mother of King Henry VI; the Founder of Eton College and King's College, Cambridge.

The Queen Catherine de Valois Society continues the tradition of prayer, begun by 15th-century pilgrims, on Queen Catherine's birthday (27 October), and the veneration of the Queen that Samuel Pepys participated in, and describes, in his diaries in 1669. Through Professor the Lord Alton and Monsignor Andrew Summersgill, the request for an Apostolic Blessing on Queen Catherine was conveyed to the Holy See.

The Society is also historical in nature, and numbers several descendants of Queen Catherine; as well as historians, architects, and other scholars. It is hoped to provide funds for the restoration of the Chapel, according to the wishes and procedures of the Abbey authorities.

A Dinner in Celebration of the State Visit was held by the Society, at the National Liberal Club, on Friday 17 September 2010, with speeches from the President, Vice-President, Prince Milan Glendza Petrovic Njegos; together with a description of his miraculous healing by the Guest of Honour, Deacon Jack Sullivan.

A REFLECTION

**The Right Reverend Dr Joe Aldred
Bishop and Secretary, Minority Ethnic
Christian Affairs, Churches Together
in England**

A Reflection on Evening Prayer in Westminster Abbey

An unheralded feature of the 2010 Papal Visit to the United Kingdom was the multi-racial makeup of the people who came out to meet him wherever he went. I was privileged to witness this as a member of the congregation in Westminster Abbey.

A significant portion of this rich tapestry of ethnicities was made up by Catholics of Africa, Caribbean and Asian heritage; which is not surprising given the Catholic Church's long-established roots in those parts of the world. Research shows that 7.6 per cent of the British Catholic community are of African, Asian or Caribbean descent (CAFOD/Ipsos Mori 2008).

I discovered that some Black and Asian people who were engaging excitedly with the Papal Visit were not Catholics at all, but were Christians from other communities, including Pentecostals.

This embrace of the Papal Visit by non-Catholics was highlighted in a press statement issued by Churches Together in England, where national church leaders welcomed the visit at a timely moment for the Christian Gospel and Church in this country. This solidarity was particularly evident at the Westminster Abbey Evening Prayer, with many key leaders and lay people from Britain's Black-led and Asian churches present.

Coming mainly from Evangelical and Pentecostal backgrounds, Black and Asian Christians also welcomed the Pope's challenge not to allow the Christian faith to become sidelined in this country.

As an ecumenist, a highlight for me was the sight of the Pope and the Archbishop of Canterbury leading worship together in Westminster Abbey. This act felt symbolically important for Christian unity.

The route to full visible unity may be known only to God, but this Papal Visit provided an opportunity for us in our diversity to affirm the prayer of Jesus that His Church may be one, that the world may believe.

Some have expressed the hope that this event will be the catalyst for closer relations between the Catholic Church in Britain and its non-Catholic neighbours in Black-led and Asian churches. This is my prayer too.

Pope Benedict XVI held a private meeting with Prime Minister David Cameron at Archbishop's House, Westminster, on Saturday 18 September 2010. The Deputy Prime Minister Nick Clegg, and the Acting Leader of the Opposition, Harriet Harman paid courtesy calls on Pope Benedict.

THE HISTORY OF WESTMINSTER CATHEDRAL

by The Reverend Father Alexander Master

Westminster Cathedral, the Metropolitan Cathedral of the Most Precious Blood, is the mother church of the Catholic Church in England and Wales. It is the focal point for major occasions in the life of the Church, both nationally and within the Archdiocese of Westminster.

The Cathedral is also the seat of the Archbishop of Westminster. Cardinal Nicholas Wiseman was the first Archbishop, being appointed at the Restoration of the Hierarchy in 1850. His successors have included Cardinals Arthur Hinsley, John Carmel Heenan, George Basil Hume, and Cormac Murphy-O'Connor. Archbishop Vincent Nichols was installed as eleventh Archbishop of Westminster on 21 May 2009.

The building of the Cathedral owes much to the energy and vision of Cardinal Herbert Vaughan, the third Archbishop of Westminster. The first stone was laid in 1895; the fabric was completed and the first regular celebrations of Mass and the Divine Office held in 1903; and the Cathedral celebrated the centenary of the consecration earlier this year.

The architectural masterwork of John Francis Bentley, the Cathedral is built in an early Christian Byzantine style – an approach which allowed the structure to be erected in a comparatively short time. The vision for the interior, envisaged from the outset of the Cathedral's planning, is one of rich decoration in mosaic and marble. There are already over 120 different varieties of marble, brought from 24 different countries, installed in the Cathedral, and many of the side-chapels have been adorned with mosaic decoration.

The visit of Pope John Paul II to the Cathedral in 1982 is commemorated by a stone set at the foot of the steps into the sanctuary.

The Cathedral Choir is justifiably world-famous. It was the wish of Cardinal Vaughan that the dignity of the building should be matched by the nobility of the liturgy and the best of music – an aim shared by Sir Richard Terry, the first Master of Music, and nurtured by those who have followed him over the decades, and who together have established the choral tradition at Westminster Cathedral as amongst the finest in the world. The choir is well-known for its recordings and has toured extensively, but its focus remains the celebration of Mass and the Divine Office.

Westminster Cathedral is a community of faith, welcoming many thousands through its doors each week. Many come to receive the Sacraments: to attend Mass, or as parishioners participating in the various sacramental programmes. A priest is always available to celebrate the Sacrament of Reconciliation with many who come to find pardon and peace from God in the Cathedral. Others come simply to find the peace and stillness which is still to be enjoyed at quieter times of day, a valuable commodity amongst the noise and business of central London.

The late George Basil, Cardinal Hume wrote, 'The remarkable creation which is Westminster Cathedral exists to help us search for God and to offer him worship. It is a home for all. It is a place where we meet Christ, and, in and through Him, gain strength and courage to take another step along the road to God.'

A glimpse at the eastern exterior of John Francis Bentley's Cathedral

THE CELEBRATION OF MASS IN WESTMINSTER CATHEDRAL

**The Most Reverend Vincent Nichols
Archbishop of Westminster
The Welcome Address given to
His Holiness Pope Benedict XVI**

*Westminster Cathedral
10.45 pm Saturday 18 September 2010*

Most Holy Father,

It is difficult to find words to express our joy and happiness at your presence here among us. You are most welcome.

I know I speak for everyone in this great congregation, drawn from every diocese in our countries and for so many who are participating by radio and television, as I express these words of greeting.

Holy Father, we offer you our love and prayers to help and sustain you in your ministry as the successor of Saint Peter. Your ministry is a great gift to us, for the Lord asks you to strengthen and nourish us, His people. That is what you do, being a sign and servant of the unity of the whole Church. Standing in the shoes of the Fisherman is demanding. So we give you our loving loyalty and sincere devotion.

Today, we are full of joy that you lead us in the celebration of the Holy Mass in this Cathedral of the Most Precious Blood of our Saviour. We come to Him because we know we stand in need of His forgiveness and healing. Wonderfully, we find these gifts opened for us in His death on the Cross. For in dying, He, who alone is God in our flesh, destroys every death that threatens us and restores our life. This is our faith, the faith of the Church, the faith which you affirm and proclaim with such authority, integrity and eloquence.

Holy Father, thank you for coming to be with us. Please lead us to the Lord, in Word and Sacrament, that He may strengthen and renew us.

Archbishop Vincent Nichols welcomes the Holy Father to Westminster Cathedral

One of the greatest challenges facing us today is how to speak convincingly of the wisdom and liberating power of God's word to a world which all too often sees the Gospel as a constriction of human freedom, instead of the truth which liberates our minds and enlightens our efforts to live wisely and well.

- Pope Benedict XVI

THE HOMILY OF THE HOLY FATHER AT WESTMINSTER CATHEDRAL

His Holiness Pope Benedict XVI's Homily given at Westminster Cathedral

Westminster Cathedral
11:00 am Saturday 18 September 2010

Dear Friends in Christ,

I greet all of you with joy in the Lord and I thank you for your warm reception. I am grateful to Archbishop Nichols for his words of welcome on your behalf. Truly, in this meeting of the Successor of Peter and the faithful of Britain, 'heart speaks unto heart' as we rejoice in the love of Christ and in our common profession of the Catholic faith which comes to us from the Apostles. I am especially happy that our meeting takes place in this Cathedral dedicated to the Most Precious Blood, which is the sign of God's redemptive mercy poured out upon the world through the passion, death and resurrection of his Son, our Lord Jesus Christ. In a particular way I greet the Archbishop of Canterbury, who honours us by his presence.

The Byzantine glory of Westminster Cathedral

The glittering Papal procession to the altar

The visitor to this Cathedral cannot fail to be struck by the great crucifix dominating the nave, which portrays Christ's body, crushed by suffering, overwhelmed by sorrow, the innocent victim whose death has reconciled us with the Father and given us a share in the very life of God. The Lord's outstretched arms seem to embrace this entire church, lifting up to the Father all the ranks of the faithful who gather around the altar of the Eucharistic sacrifice and share in its fruits. The crucified Lord stands above and before us as the source of our life and salvation, 'the high priest of the good things to come', as the author of the Letter to the Hebrews calls him in today's first reading (Heb 9:11).

It is in the shadow, so to speak, of this striking image, that I would like to consider the word of God which has been proclaimed in our midst and reflect on the mystery of the Precious Blood. For that mystery leads us to see the unity between

Christ's sacrifice on the Cross, the Eucharistic sacrifice which he has given to his Church, and his eternal priesthood, whereby, seated at the right hand of the Father, he makes unceasing intercession for us, the members of his mystical body.

Let us begin with the sacrifice of the Cross. The outpouring of Christ's blood is the source of the Church's life. Saint John, as we know, sees in the water and blood which flowed from our Lord's body the wellspring of that divine life which is bestowed by the Holy Spirit and communicated to us in the sacraments (Jn 19:34; cf. 1 Jn 1:7; 5:6-7). The Letter to the Hebrews draws out, we might say, the liturgical implications of this mystery. Jesus, by his suffering and death, his self-oblation in the eternal Spirit, has become our high priest and 'the mediator of a new covenant' (Heb 9:15). These words echo our Lord's own words at the Last Supper, when he instituted the Eucharist as the sacrament of his body, given up for us, and his blood, the blood of the new and everlasting covenant shed for the forgiveness of sins (cf. Mk 14:24; Mt 26:28; Lk 22:20).

Faithful to Christ's command to 'do this in memory of me' (Lk 22:19), the Church in every time and place celebrates the Eucharist until the Lord returns in glory, rejoicing in his sacramental presence and drawing upon the power of his saving sacrifice for the redemption of the world. The reality of the Eucharistic sacrifice has always been at the heart of Catholic faith; called into question in the 16th century, it was solemnly reaffirmed at the Council of Trent against the backdrop of our justification in Christ. Here in England, as we know, there were many who staunchly defended the Mass, often at great cost, giving rise to that devotion to the Most Holy Eucharist which has been a hallmark of Catholicism in these lands.

The Eucharistic sacrifice of the Body and Blood of Christ embraces in turn the mystery of our Lord's continuing passion in the members of his Mystical Body, the Church in every age. Here the great crucifix which towers above us serves as a reminder that Christ, our eternal high priest, daily unites our own sacrifices, our own sufferings, our own needs, hopes and aspirations, to the infinite merits of his sacrifice. Through him, with him, and in him, we lift up our own bodies as a sacrifice holy and acceptable to God (cf. Rom 12:1). In this sense we are caught up in his eternal oblation, completing, as Saint Paul says, in our flesh what is lacking in Christ's afflictions for the sake of

Pope Benedict stands at the archiepiscopal throne

his body, the Church (cf. Col 1:24). In the life of the Church, in her trials and tribulations, Christ continues, in the stark phrase of Pascal, 'to be in agony until the end of the world' (*Pensées*, 553, éd. Brunschvicg).

We see this aspect of the mystery of Christ's precious blood represented, most eloquently, by the martyrs of every age, who drank from the cup which Christ himself drank, and whose own blood, shed in union with his sacrifice, gives new life to the Church. It is also reflected in our brothers and sisters throughout the world who even now are suffering discrimination and persecution for their Christian faith. Yet it is also present, often hidden in the suffering of all those individual Christians who daily unite their sacrifices to those of the Lord for the sanctification of the Church and the redemption of the world. My thoughts go in a special way to all those who are spiritually united with this Eucharistic celebration, and in particular the sick, the elderly, the handicapped and those who suffer mentally and spiritually.

Here too, I think of the immense suffering caused by the abuse of children, especially within the Church and by her ministers. Above all, I express my deep sorrow to the innocent victims of these unspeakable crimes, along with my hope that the power of Christ's grace, his sacrifice of reconciliation, will bring deep healing and peace to their lives. I also acknowledge, with you, the shame and humiliation which all of us have suffered because of these sins; and I invite you to offer it to the Lord with trust that this chastisement will contribute to the healing of the victims, the purification of the Church and the renewal of her age-old commitment to the education and care of young people. I express my gratitude for the efforts being made to address this problem responsibly, and I ask all of you to show your concern for the victims and solidarity with your priests.

Dear friends, let us return to the contemplation of the great crucifix which rises above us. Our Lord's hands, extended on the Cross, also invite us to contemplate our participation in his eternal priesthood and thus our responsibility, as members of his body, to bring the reconciling power of his sacrifice to the world in which we live. The

Second Vatican Council spoke eloquently of the indispensable role of the laity in carrying forward the Church's mission through their efforts to serve as a leaven of the Gospel in society and to work for the advancement of God's Kingdom in the world (cf. *Lumen Gentium*, 31; *Apostolicam Actuositatem*, 7). The Council's appeal to the lay faithful to take up their baptismal sharing in Christ's mission echoed the insights and teachings of John Henry Newman. May the profound ideas of this great Englishman continue to inspire all Christ's followers in this land to conform their every thought, word and action to Christ, and to work strenuously to defend those unchanging moral truths which, taken up, illuminated and confirmed by the Gospel, stand at the foundation of a truly humane, just and free society.

How much contemporary society needs this witness! How much we need, in the Church and in society, witnesses of the beauty of holiness, witnesses of the splendour of truth, witnesses of the joy and freedom born of a living relationship with Christ! One of the greatest challenges facing us today is how to speak convincingly of the wisdom and liberating power of God's word to a world which all too often sees the Gospel as a constriction of human freedom, instead of the truth which liberates our minds and enlightens our

His Holiness raises the chalice in this Cathedral of the Most Precious Blood

efforts to live wisely and well, both as individuals and as members of society.

Let us pray, then, that the Catholics of this land will become ever more conscious of their dignity as a priestly people, called to consecrate the world to God through lives of faith and holiness. And may this increase of apostolic zeal be accompanied by an outpouring of prayer for vocations to the ordained priesthood. For the more the lay apostolate grows, the more urgently the need for priests is felt; and the more the laity's own sense of vocation is deepened, the more what is proper to the priest stands out. May many young men in this land find the strength to answer the Master's call to the ministerial priesthood, devoting their lives, their energy and their talents to God, thus building up his people in unity and fidelity to the Gospel, especially through the celebration of the Eucharistic sacrifice.

Dear friends, in this Cathedral of the Most Precious Blood, I invite you once more to look to Christ, who leads us in our faith and brings it to perfection (cf. Heb 12:2). I ask you to unite yourselves ever more fully to the Lord, sharing in his sacrifice on the Cross and offering him that 'spiritual worship' (Rom 12:1) which embraces every aspect of our lives and finds expression in our efforts to contribute to the coming of his Kingdom. I pray that, in doing so, you may join the ranks of faithful believers throughout the long Christian history of this land, in building a society truly worthy of man, worthy of your nation's highest traditions.

How much we need, in the Church and in society, witnesses of the beauty of holiness, witnesses of the splendour of truth, witnesses of the joy and freedom born of a living relationship with Christ!

- Pope Benedict XVI

Pope Benedict XVI, bishops and others in the Cathedral sacristy

A blessing for those who came bearing gifts

Cardinal Cormac Murphy-O'Connor and Archbishop Vincent Nichols concelebrating the Mass with the Holy Father

YOUNG PEOPLE WELCOME HIS HOLINESS POPE BENEDICT XVI

Welcome given to the Holy Father on behalf of Young People in the United Kingdom

Welcome to His Holiness Pope Benedict XVI on behalf of the young people of England, Wales and Scotland by Mr Paschal Uche.
12:00 pm Saturday 18 September 2010

Dear Holy Father,

It is a privilege and a great pleasure to welcome you on behalf of young Catholics from England, Wales and Scotland. Your visit brings us together - it is like a family reunion - and we are very pleased to see you.

My name is Paschal Uche and I am from St Francis' Parish in East London. Gathered here today are 2500 young people representing almost every parish in the country. Like many here, I have been actively involved in the Church, serving the elderly in Lourdes and going on retreat. I know that others help in Confirmation sessions, parish music groups, youth groups, and projects serving those who are disadvantaged. We are a truly living Church that offers great opportunities for young people to encounter the love of Christ and share it.

Pope John Paul II said that our faith is a 'noble and authentic adventure' and we really want other young people to experience this. It is our prayer that your visit inspires us to be 'saints of the third millennium.'

Holy Father, we would like to ask you to bless for us a candle stand, which we hope will be a symbol for Catholic Youth Ministry. It has been thoughtfully designed for use in prayer, teaching and meditation.

For many of us, before today, you were a face on the television or a picture in a church, but today we behold you face-to-face, and on behalf of the Catholic youth of this great nation, I would like to express my profound and heartfelt gratitude for your visit. May God Bless You.

THE ADDRESS OF THE HOLY FATHER TO YOUNG PEOPLE

His Holiness Pope Benedict XVI's Message to Young People

Westminster Cathedral Piazza
12:10 pm Saturday 18 September 2010

Mr Uche, dear young friends, thank you for your warm welcome.

'Heart Speaks unto heart'; as you know, I chose these words so dear to Cardinal Newman, as the theme of my visit. In these few moments that we are together, I wish to speak to you from my own heart, and I ask you to open your hearts to what I have to say.

I ask each of you first and foremost to look into your own heart, think of all the love that your heart was made to receive, and also, of the love it is meant to give, after all we were made for love. This is what the Bible means when it says

A smiling Holy Father greets his young audience

that we are made in the image and likeness of God. We were made to know the God of love, the God who is Father, Son and Holy Spirit, and to find our supreme fulfilment in that Divine love that knows no beginning or end.

We were made to receive love, and we have. Every day, we should thank God for the love we have already known. For the love that has made us who we are. The love that has shown us what is truly important in life. We need to thank the Lord for the love we have received from our families, our friends, our teachers, and all those people in our lives who have helped us to realise how precious we are in their eyes, and in the eyes of God.

We were also made to give love, to make it the inspiration for all we do, and the most enduring thing in our lives. At times, it seems so natural, especially when we feel the exhilaration of love, when our hearts brim over with generosity, idealism, the desire to help others to build a better

The young people waiting to see the Holy Father outside Westminster Cathedral

Grace which he bestows on us in the sacraments of his Church. This is the message I want to share with you today. I ask you to look into your hearts, each day, to find the source of all true love. Jesus is always there. Quietly waiting for us to be still with him and to hear his voice. Deep within your heart, he is calling you to spend time with him in prayer, but this kind of prayer, real prayer, requires discipline.

It requires time for moments of silence every day. Often it means waiting for the Lord to speak.

Even amidst the business and stress of our daily lives, we need to make space for silence, because it is in silence that we find God. And in silence that we discover our true self.

And in discovering our true self we discover the particular vocation which God has given us for the building up of his Church and the redemption of our world. *'Heart speaks unto heart'*. With these words from my heart, dear young friends, I assure you of my prayers for you.

That our lives will bear fruit of the cross, of the civilisation of the cross, I ask you to pray for me, for my Ministry as the successor of Peter, and for the needs of the Church throughout the world. Upon you, your families and friends, I call on you God's blessing of wisdom, joy and peace.

world - but at other times, we realise it is difficult to love. Our hearts can easily be hardened by selfishness, envy and pride. The Blessed Mother Theresa of Calcutta, the great missionary of charity, reminded us that giving love; pure and generous love, is the fruit of a daily decision.

Every day, we have to choose to love and this requires help. The help that comes from Christ, from the wisdom found in his word, and from the

A REFLECTION

The Reverend Canon Christopher Tuckwell, Administrator of Westminster Cathedral

A Reflection on Mass in Westminster Cathedral with special reference to the Centenary Year of Westminster Cathedral

For several months, it seemed as though there was almost nothing else on our minds than the visit of the Holy Father to the country as a whole, but more specifically to Westminster Cathedral.

In the last few weeks the details had all been coming together with the preparation of the floor-plan, the detailing of stewards and volunteers and the practising of altar-servers. In the last few days the men from the BBC set up their lighting and equipment, the florists laid out their arrangements and the statue of Our Lady of Cardigan arrived, until at last all seemed ready.

When the Holy Father arrived in the Outer Sacristy, despite all the preparations, it almost seemed unreal. Was the Pope actually here? He was indeed, and he brought a beautiful sense of calm and peace, and his unhurried, prayerful attention to the liturgy permeated the whole celebration.

The particularly special moments for me were the powerful and thoughtful words of his homily; the two profound silences after the homily and after Communion; the dignified and yet homely moment when he blessed the new mosaic of Saint David and spoke specifically to the people of Wales; and the brief personal meeting granted to the Provost and myself.

The moment which stands out above all for me was the opening of the West Doors and the roar of welcome from the young people gathered on the Piazza – that was the moment that really brought a lump to my throat. What a privilege in the Centenary Year of the Cathedral's Consecration to be welcoming the Holy Father to this great house of prayer in the heart of London.

CHRISTIANITY IN WALES

by the Right Reverend Daniel Mullins

When, in 383, *Magnus Maximus withdrew the regular defences of the Province in pursuit of his claim to the imperial crown, the West of Britain lacked large Roman towns.* This would determine the subsequent ecclesiastical structures in the city-less parts of Britain, including in what is now Wales.

The Church was organised more around monastic communities than in territorial dioceses. In the 6th century, monasticism would become the driving force for a re-evangelisation of the people of Wales. In Wales the 6th century is remembered as the Age of the Saints of Illtud, Teilo, Padarn, of Saint David and their many companions still honoured in the Church calendar for Wales.

By the time of the Norman invasion, this older monastic structure had become static and much of church administration was in the hands of laymen. In a spirit of renewal and reform, newer Religious Orders came to Wales.

The Cistercian Order took root and became a part of the fabric of Welsh life. The orders of Friars and especially the Dominicans and Franciscans brought the reforms of the Fourth Lateran Council, reforms that would have a profound effect on Welsh culture and on the production of manuscript collections of both secular and sacred writings.

The accepted view among historians is that the Reformation was not welcomed in Wales, but that by the end of Elizabeth's reign, Wales had become a Protestant nation. This opinion requires closer examination. Among the Cecil papers at Hatfield, is a letter dated 1603, from a judge in the Recusant courts, lamenting that Wales is still steeped in superstition and popery. Even in the time of King Charles II, Wales is listed as one of the four strongholds of Catholicism.

In 1536, an Act usually known as the Act of Union decreed that Wales should be 'incorporated, united and annexed' to the realm of England. In 1579, Owen Lewis would write to Cardinal Sirleto appealing for funds to print religious works

St David (c500-589). Stained-glass window at Saint David's Cathedral in South Wales

Raglan Castle, Monmouthshire in Wales, seat of the Somerset family

in Welsh. The Welsh exiles on the continent were very clear that Wales needed different treatment from England, if the Faith were to survive there. Such an approach met with little understanding in Rome, or elsewhere.

Catholicism did survive strongly in the Monmouthshire area, due in large measure to the influence of the Somerset family of Raglan Castle. Edward Somerset, (4th) Earl of Worcester (1553-1628) was a proud Welshman who used the Welsh language and saw it as a key to the pastoral work of his age. Described as a 'stiff papist who was also a loyal subject', he settled Catholic families from Glamorganshire and from different areas of England on his lands. He helped establish the College of St Francis on the Monmouth/Hereford border and was sufficiently confident in 1615 to register the lease in the name of the Jesuit Superior. His influence explains why the English county of Herefordshire still today comes within the ecclesiastical Province of Cardiff. Until 1679, the College was the spearhead of the Jesuit mission in Wales.

In 1767, Charles Walmesley sent a report on the Western District to the Vatican Office of Propaganda Fidei. The statistics given for Herefordshire were of 190 Catholics served by seven missionaries. The whole of Wales was said to have 750 Catholics and

nine missionaries. In the information sent to Rome prior to the establishment of the Welsh District in 1840, the area had a total of 17 priests and 6,519 Catholics. The following decade saw a further big increase in numbers, due to the Irish Famine and subsequent migration.

In the Restoration of the Hierarchy in 1850, Herefordshire and the southern counties of Wales were formed into the Diocese of Newport and Menevia; the six counties of North Wales formed part of the Diocese of Shrewsbury.

On becoming Archbishop of Westminster in 1892, Cardinal Vaughan insisted that the religious needs of Wales were distinct from those of England and therefore required to be treated separately. In 1895 the three counties of Glamorganshire, Monmouthshire and Herefordshire became the Diocese of Newport; the remaining counties became the Vicariate of Wales. In 1898, this became the Diocese of Menevia. The Cardinal did not live to see the erection of the Province of Cardiff in 1916 and the establishment of a Welsh Hierarchy.

In 1987, a further reorganisation saw the creation of a third diocese. Menevia was restored to what was very nearly its medieval territory and the Diocese of Wrexham was formed.

THE CATHOLIC CHURCH IN WALES

The Right Reverend Edwin Regan, Bishop of Wrexham, Official Welcome to His Holiness Pope Benedict XVI on behalf of the People of Wales

Westminster Cathedral, Chapel of St Paul
12:30 pm Saturday 18 September 2010

Your Holiness,

On behalf of the Catholics of Wales, and of Wales itself, I am immensely privileged to offer you our most sincere sentiments of loving respect and deep appreciation of all that you do, for the building of God's Kingdom on earth.

Our joy that you are here in Britain is tempered by our disappointment that you cannot visit Wales on this occasion. But that regret is itself a sign of our esteem for you and your ministry of love in truth, *'Caritas in Veritate'*.

We are delighted that you are reaching out to Wales by lighting the candle held by Our Lady of Cardigan as she presents to us her Son, as the light of the world.

That light is reflected to us by all those who have lived open to God's love, people who are represented by Saint David, the Patron Saint of Wales. In blessing this mosaic dedicated to Saint David, you remind modern Wales that we must not forget the Christian values that formed this nation of Wales throughout its history.

Dad Sanctaidd, ar ran Catholigion Cymru, a Chymru ei hun, mae hi'n fraint arbennig iawn i mi allu cyflwyno i chi ein teimladau diffuant o barch cariadus, a gwerthfawrogiad dwys o'r hyn rydych chi'n ei gyflawni i adeiladu teyrnas Dduw ar y ddaear.

Mae ein llawenydd yn cael ei dymheru gan ein siom nad ydych yn gallu ymweld â Chymru y tro hwn. Ond mae'r siom hwnnw, ynddo'i hun, yn arwydd o'n hedmygedd ohonoch ac o'ch gweinidogaeth o gariad mewn gwirionedd, *Caritas in Veritate*.

Rydym yn falch iawn eich bod yn ymestyn tuag at Gymru trwy gynnau'r gannwyll a ddelir gan Ein Harglwyddes o Aberteifi wrth iddi gyflwyno'i Mab fel goleuni'r byd.

Mae'r goleuni hwnnw yn cael ei adlewyrchu atom gan bawb sydd wedi byw bywyd sy'n agored i gariad Duw, pobl a gynrychiolir gan Dewi Sant, Nawddsant ein gwlad. Wrth fendithio'r mosaig yma a gysegrir i Ddewi, rydych yn atgoffa Cymru heddiw na ddylem fyth anghofio'r gwerthoedd Cristnogol a ffurfiodd genedl y Cymry trwy gydol ei hanes.

THE GREETING BY THE HOLY FATHER TO THE PEOPLE OF WALES

The Greeting given by the Holy Father to the Faithful of Wales

Westminster Cathedral, Chapel of St Paul
12:30 pm Saturday 18 September 2010

Dear Bishop Regan,

Thank you for your very warm greeting on behalf of the faithful of Wales. I am happy to have this opportunity to honour the nation and its ancient Christian traditions, by blessing a mosaic of Saint David, the patron saint of the Welsh people, and by lighting the candle of the statue of Our Lady of Cardigan.

Saint David was one of the great saints of the 6th century, that golden age of saints and missionaries in these isles, and he was thus a founder of the Christian culture which lies at the root of modern Europe. David's preaching was simple yet profound: his dying words to his monks were, 'Be joyful, keep the faith, and do the little things'. It is the little things that reveal our love for the one who loved us first (cf. 1 Jn 4:19) and that bind people into a community of faith, love and service. May Saint David's message, in all its simplicity and richness, continue to resound in Wales today, drawing the hearts of its people to renewed love for Christ and his Church.

Through the ages the Welsh people have been distinguished for their devotion to the Mother of God; this is evidenced by the innumerable places in Wales called 'Llanfair' – 'Mary's Church'. As I prepare to light the candle held by Our Lady, I pray that she will continue to intercede with her Son for all the men and women of Wales. May the light of Christ continue to guide their steps and shape the life and culture of the nation.

Sadly, it was not possible for me to come to Wales during this visit, but I trust that this beautiful statue, which now returns to the National Shrine of Our Lady in Cardigan, will be a lasting reminder of the Pope's deep love for the Welsh people, and of his constant closeness, both in prayer and in the communion of the Church.

Bendith Duw ar bobol Cymru! God bless the people of Wales!

Bishop of Wrexham, Edwin Regan, welcomes the Holy Father on behalf of the people of Wales

I have great pleasure in presenting to Your Holiness a striking reminder of those who have gone before us. Blessed William Davies wrote a book of Catholic devotion called '*Y Drych Cristionogawl*' - '*The Christian Mirror*', which was the first book published in Wales. The romantic story of its being printed in a cave on a remote seashore has entered the folklore of Wales, and it speaks to us of a people who loved the Catholic Faith, and were prepared to sacrifice all for the one thing necessary, the love of God in truth.

This facsimile printed this year, of a book printed in 1588, calls us to the same witness as we see in the lives of Blessed William Davies and the other Welsh Martyrs, both Catholic and Protestant.

- *The Right Reverend Edwin Regan*

The Pope blesses the new mosaic of Saint David. Below, left, the statue of Our Lady of Cardigan, whose taper (candle) the Holy Father has just lit

A REFLECTION

The Reverend Monsignor Peter M Brignall, Cathedral Dean of Our Lady of Sorrows, Wrexham, and Vicar General of the Diocese of Wrexham

A Reflection on the celebration of Mass, the Blessing of the mosaic of Saint David and the lighting of the taper of Our Lady of Cardigan in Westminster Cathedral

In the closing words of his Homily, the Holy Father gave recognition and paid tribute to 'the ranks of faithful believers throughout the long Christian history of this land' as he invited us all to unite ourselves more fully to the Lord in faithful discipleship today.

In the silence that followed, I was minded to think of Saint Boniface. Boniface was a monk of mixed Anglo-Saxon/British blood who left our shores to take the Gospel to Germanic Europe. Now I was one among the bishops and priests of England and Wales celebrating Mass with a Pope from Bavaria in London. This was all the more poignant as I reflected that it was through my German mother that the gift of faith was given to me, truly reason enough to be thankful and celebrate.

Little was I to know that an hour later, Pope Benedict, when he came to bless the new mosaic of Saint David in the side chapel close to the great pulpit in the Cathedral, would refer to 'that golden age of saints and missionaries of these isles, [who were founders] of the Christian culture which lies at the root of modern Europe' among whom Saint David numbers.

Boniface would have known and felt Saint David's influence from a hundred years earlier. As the Holy Father spoke and echoed my own thoughts, I realised again how a number of seemingly unconnected incidents or events in our lives, like the different cut stones and tiles of a mosaic, come together to form the beauty of the whole. The two other pieces that complete this Reflection, are that I was ordained deacon in Westminster Cathedral and that I have lived my life as a priest in Wales.

The Holy Father's gracious words to Bishop Regan and to the people of Wales at the blessing of the mosaic of Saint David and the lighting of the taper of the statue of Our Lady of Cardigan, were a clarion call to the Church and to the world of that long Christian heritage in which we are to be proud, to which we are to witness, and in which we are to rejoice.

This part of the Pope's visit to the United Kingdom was as profound, as splendid and as inspiring as one could have hoped or expected.

Bendith Duw ar bobol Cymru! God bless the people of Wales!

God bless Pope Benedict XVI!

THE VISIT TO ST PETER'S RESIDENCE FOR OLDER PEOPLE

Sister Marie Claire Brennan welcomes His Holiness Pope Benedict XVI to St Peter's Residence

St Peter's Residence, Vauxhall
5:20 pm Saturday 18 September 2010

Most Holy Father,

It is with great joy in our hearts that we say 'Welcome Holy Father; welcome to St Peter's Residence'. Our joy is born of gratitude and thanksgiving to God for the immense privilege that is ours today, and so, in the name of Mother General, the Little Sisters of the Poor and residents here at St Peter's and all over the world we assure you of our love, our deep affection and, above all, our prayers.

You have come in the name of Christ and his Church to confirm and strengthen us in our faith, so it is with eager anticipation that we await the message you are about to address to us.

It is in visiting your elderly brothers and sisters that you bear special witness to the immeasurable love of the Heart of Jesus for some of the most vulnerable and often frail members of today's society. Thank you, Holy Father, for including this visit to older people in your agenda. By doing so, you are underlining the real importance of caring for the elderly in our world of today.

Each elderly person has a vast experience of life, with their own story to tell. Often they have accumulated a great store of wisdom and strength of character and we know that the life of each one is precious in the eyes of God.

We are really happy to assure you, Holy Father, that each day here in St Peter's and in our Homes throughout the world, our Residents and Sisters pray very specially for your intentions and for the needs of the Church. You will notice that we are very blessed to have our Resident Priests who contribute so much spiritually, not only to our home but also to the life of the Church through the joyful and faithful witness they give of their Priesthood.

Little Sister of the Poor Sister Marie Claire Brennan, who welcomed Pope Benedict XVI to St Peter's Residence.

We recall with great happiness and deep appreciation the Canonisation of our Foundress, Saint Jeanne Jugan, in Rome, on 11 October last year. Her message of love, respect and care of the elderly is more actual than ever in today's society. On that day, Holy Father, when referring to Saint Jeanne Jugan, you greatly encouraged us with these words:

'Her charism is ever timely while so many elderly people are suffering from numerous forms of poverty and solitude... May Saint Jeanne Jugan be for elderly people a living source of hope.'

May we, her daughters, always cherish her charism and follow, with a spirit of love and generosity, in her footsteps.

Thank you, Holy Father, for showing us your loving concern for the elderly. Thank you from the bottom of our hearts for being here with us today. Your visit will always remain a source of immense joy and something we shall treasure for the rest of our lives!

Welcome Holy Father.

Mrs Fasky's Welcome to His Holiness Pope Benedict XVI

St Peter's Residence, Vauxhall
5:23 pm Saturday 18 September 2010

Dear Holy Father,

All the residents here in St Peter's are tremendously honoured that you have chosen to come to us today. It is such a great privilege! Thank you for showing your care for us.

We always listen for your words of encouragement to the elderly all over the world. They are a great source of comfort and inspiration.

Holy Father, we all love you.

Thank you and once again welcome.

Saint Jeanne Jugan

In a small fishing village in Brittany, France, on 25 October 1792, Jeanne Jugan was born. By the time of her death, in 1879 a little community which she had founded in 1839 to care for the most pitiful of poor and abandoned older women had grown to 2,400 sisters, their houses spread across Europe and beyond.

What community was this? They were, and are, the Little Sisters of the Poor. The icon, left, captures Jeanne Jugan in her lifelong posture of loving care for the less fortunate.

Jeanne was 47 when she began to serve and to share in the sufferings of the poor, even their physical sufferings. She considered herself one of them. And it was as their numbers grew that the number of her sisters grew, accepting the simple rule Jeanne proposed for them and for herself.

This sweet-souled Servant of God was beatified in Rome on 3 October 1982 by Pope John Paul II and canonised on 9 October 2009 by Pope Benedict XVI.

THE ADDRESS OF THE HOLY FATHER

His Holiness Pope Benedict XVI's Speech to the Residents and Staff of St Peter's

St Peter's Residence, Vauxhall
5:25 pm Saturday 18 September 2010

My dear Brothers and Sisters,

I am very pleased to be among you, the residents of St Peter's, and to thank Sister Marie Claire and Mrs Fasky for their kind words of welcome on your behalf. I am also pleased to greet Archbishop Smith of Southwark, as well as the Little Sisters of the Poor and the personnel and volunteers who look after you.

As advances in medicine and other factors lead to increased longevity, it is important to recognise the presence of growing numbers of older people as a blessing for society. Every generation can learn from the experience and wisdom of the generation that preceded it. Indeed, the provision of care for the elderly should be considered not so much an act of generosity as the repayment of a debt of gratitude.

For her part, the Church has always had great respect for the elderly. The Fourth Commandment, 'Honour your father and your mother as the Lord your God commanded you' (Deut 5:16), is linked to the promise, 'that your days may be prolonged, and that it may go well with you, in the land which the Lord your God gives you' (Deut 5:16). This work of the Church for the aging and infirm not only provides love and care for them, but is also rewarded by God with the blessings he

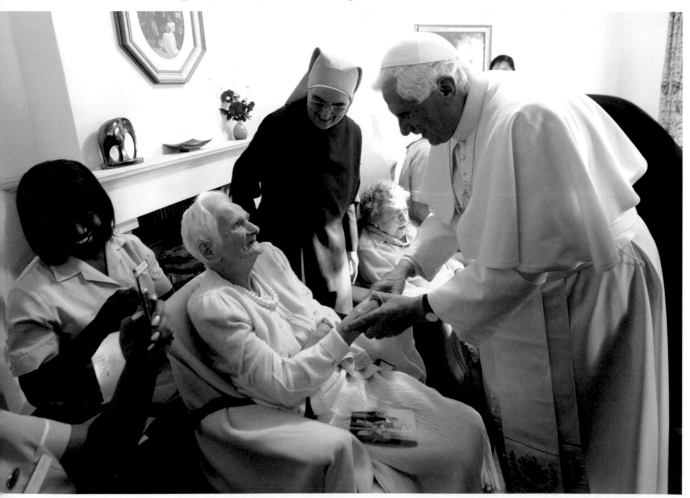

Pope Benedict greets an older resident with affection

Pope Benedict, Cardinal Bertone and Archbishop Peter Smith

promises on the land where this commandment is observed. God wills a proper respect for the dignity and worth, the health and well-being of the elderly and, through her charitable institutions in Britain and beyond, the Church seeks to fulfil the Lord's command to respect life, regardless of age or circumstances.

At the very start of my pontificate I said, 'Each of us is willed, each of us is loved, each of us is necessary' (Homily at the Mass for the Beginning of the Petrine Ministry of the Bishop of Rome, 24 April 2005). Life is a unique gift, at every stage from conception until natural death, and it is God's alone to give and to take. One may enjoy good health in old age; but equally Christians should not be afraid to share in the suffering of Christ, if God wills that we struggle with infirmity. My predecessor, the late Pope John Paul, suffered very publicly during the last years of his life. It was clear to all of us that he did so in union with the sufferings of our Saviour. His cheerfulness and forbearance as he faced his final days were a remarkable and moving example to all of us who have to carry the burden of advancing years.

In this sense, I come among you not only as a father, but also as a brother who knows well the joys and the struggles that come with age. Our long years of life afford us the opportunity to appreciate both the beauty of God's greatest gift to us, the gift of life, as well as the fragility of the human spirit. Those of us who live many years are given a marvellous chance to deepen our awareness of the mystery of Christ, who humbled himself to share in our humanity. As the normal span of our lives increases, our physical capacities are often diminished; and yet these times may well be among the most spiritually fruitful years of our lives. These years are an opportunity to remember in affectionate prayer all those whom we have cherished in this life, and to place all that we have personally been and done before the mercy and tenderness of God. This will surely be a great spiritual comfort and enable us to discover anew his love and goodness all the days of our life.

With these sentiments, dear brothers and sisters, I am pleased to assure you of my prayers for you all, and I ask for your prayers for me. May our Blessed Lady and her spouse, Saint Joseph intercede for our happiness in this life and obtain for us the blessing of a serene passage to the next.

May God bless you all!

A REFLECTION

**The Most Reverend Peter Smith
Archbishop of Southwark**

A Reflection on the Pope's visit to St Peter's Residence for older people, Vauxhall, and on welcoming His Holiness to the Hyde Park Vigil

Of all the events of the Papal Visit, whether the great State occasions or the religious celebrations, my abiding memory will be of Pope Benedict's visit to St Peter's Residential Care Home, in Vauxhall. Catholics of all ages from the local community, clutching their papal flags, gathered in Meadow Road waiting with great excitement for him to arrive. They were hoping that the Holy Father would come out and greet them, and all I could say at that stage was that I would do my best to encourage him to do just that.

When Pope Benedict arrived, and after the initial introductions, the Holy Father spoke of the growing numbers of older people in society which he described as a blessing for every generation who could learn from the experience and wisdom of preceding generations. He said that in respecting the dignity, worth and well-being of the elderly, the Church seeks 'to fulfil the Lord's command to respect life, regardless of age or circumstances.'

Whether greeting the residents, or afterwards the crowds outside in the road, what came across very movingly was his graciousness, his fatherly concern and his delight in meeting ordinary people. Everyone was thrilled, especially when quite spontaneously he began to walk down Meadow Road, (much to the consternation of his Vatican Security agents), blessing the children and waving to the crowds. The reality was far away from the media caricature of the remote academic with no experience of, or concern for, ordinary life and people. This was a loving father and brother, glad to meet his family.

In Hyde Park on Saturday afternoon, around 80,000 people gathered to celebrate their faith and share their experience as pilgrims journeying through this life towards the home of their heavenly Father. That huge and cheerful gathering filled the park with processions, moving testimonies and reflections. Much joyful singing filled that enormous arena as they waited for the arrival of Pope Benedict in the early evening with great anticipation.

They gave him a rapturous welcome and the Holy Father was visibly moved by his reception. But after he had addressed the crowds, and the Prayer Vigil began before the Blessed Sacrament, there was a dramatic change of mood. The festive and noisy celebrations gave way to an extraordinary stillness and silence. It was for me an incredibly moving experience, because that prayerful stillness and silence in that vast crowd was a tangible witness of the whole theme of the visit, *'Heart speaks to Heart.'*

Here was the Church, in adoration of the Blessed Sacrament; in communion with Our Blessed Lord, in communion with the Vicar of Christ and one another, witnessing to our faith in God and in the Church Christ founded. What an extraordinary experience it was, and one which none of us there will ever forget.

A REFLECTION

**Sister Marie Claire Brennan
Little Sister of the Poor, Local Superior
of St Peter's Residence, a Care Home
for Older People**

*A Reflection made in her role as the main co-ordinator
in the preparations for the Holy Father's visit to
St Peter's Residence*

Saturday 18 September 2010 will remain forever engraved in my memory as one of the greatest graces of my life.

As I walked around the house before the Holy Father's arrival, the mounting excitement was palpable, especially amongst the residents and sisters.

In the chapel the choir was rehearsing, leading everyone in song. It was so uplifting to hear the words of the hymn 'Gather your people O Lord'… and here we were gathering together to welcome the Pope himself! In the grounds, residents' families were being entertained by two seminarians playing the violin and guitar. The atmosphere was electric. I was moved seeing the enthusiasm of everyone, even the technicians and security people.

I remember thinking: 'here we are, celebrating life, love, joy; this is what being Church is all about. It's all of us coming together as One Body, to share in this historic moment; a real celebration of God's love.'

As the Holy Father arrived, I was so excited yet strangely calm. Christ's representative on earth was here, with us. As he greeted each one, time stood still. He is a powerful yet gentle presence. I felt utterly drawn by his sincere attention to each and every person he encountered. His profound gaze spoke volumes.

Accompanying the Holy Father around the home, I witnessed the 'Gentle Christ' seeking out the poor and lowly, truly the Gospel in action.

Pope Benedict is such an example to us all. It was touching to hear him refer to himself as coming not only as a father but as a 'brother who knows well the joys and the struggles that come with age…'

His words are a powerful message, encouraging and strengthening me in my vocation, striving afresh to 'repay the debt of gratitude' we owe to each and every older person for whom we have the privilege to care.

Pope Benedict makes an impromptu stop

A REFLECTION

The Right Reverend Monsignor Martin Lee
Chaplain to St Peter's Residence

A Reflection on the visit to St Peter's Residence for older people, Vauxhall

As we began this week I found myself a muddle of anxieties and excitements. The anxieties don't matter much now, they but included whether I would be 'tongue-tied' when greeting the Pope.

Never before had such an intelligent and profound theologian come to our little backwater. A taxi driver was amazed to discover Meadow Road blocked off by the police. 'What's the Pope doing coming to a backwater like this?' he said. This is the littleness of the Little Sisters of the Poor: intelligent and profound women working away here day after day, their story untold. I felt so happy for them, that, for once, their true value was acknowledged.

The theologian and the successor to Saint Peter was going to speak to us about our contribution to the life of the Church in caring for older people. A lot more needs to be said and thought about the spiritual care of our 'elders' by Catholics, so that we can influence society to share our values. Maybe this would be a start. Well, it is a start.

For myself, I remember being taught at school that soldiers salute the rank of the officer, not the person who holds the rank, and the same is true of us in the respect we express for the priesthood of Christ. When the Pope finally arrived, I felt concentrated in that moment the truth of all the Popes in history being the bearers of the Petrine office, an office established by Christ himself when he walked on the earth. I kissed the Pope's ring and felt a bit overwhelmed. I was tongue-tied. But did it matter? I had said what I believed and felt.

His Holiness Pope Benedict XVI's Address to Safeguarding Professionals

St Peter's Residence, Vauxhall
5:45 pm Saturday 18 September 2010

Dear Friends,

I am glad to have the opportunity to greet you, who represent the many professionals and volunteers responsible for child protection in church environments. The Church has a long tradition of caring for children from their earliest years through to adulthood, following the affectionate example of Christ, who blessed the children brought to him, and who taught his disciples that to such as these 'the Kingdom of Heaven' belongs (cf. Mk 10:13-16).

Your work, carried out within the framework of the recommendations made in the first instance by the Nolan Report and subsequently by the Cumberlege Commission, has made a vital contribution to the promotion of safe environments for young people. It helps to ensure that the preventative measures put in place are effective, that they are maintained with vigilance, and that any allegations of abuse are dealt with swiftly and justly. On behalf of the many children you serve and their parents, let me thank you for the good work that you have done and continue to do in this field.

It is deplorable that, in such marked contrast to the Church's long tradition of care for them, children have suffered abuse and mistreatment at the hands of some priests and religious. We have all become much more aware of the need to safeguard children, and you are an important part of the Church's broad-ranging response to the problem. While there are never grounds for complacency, credit should be given where it is due: the efforts of the Church in this country and elsewhere, especially in the last ten years, to guarantee the safety of children and young people and to show them every respect as they grow to maturity, should be acknowledged. I pray that your generous service will help to reinforce an atmosphere of trust and renewed commitment to the welfare of children, who are such a precious gift from God.

May God prosper your work, and may he pour out his blessings upon all of you.

Huge crowds throng the Mall to catch a glimpse of the Pope

THE PRAYER VIGIL HELD UPON THE EVE OF THE BEATIFICATION OF VENERABLE JOHN HENRY NEWMAN IN HYDE PARK, LONDON

The Most Reverend Peter Smith Archbishop of Southwark, welcomes His Holiness Pope Benedict XVI to Hyde Park

7:05 pm Saturday 18 September 2010

Most Holy Father,

We welcome you this evening: from the heart of London, from the hearts of all of us here in Hyde Park, and from the hearts of all those united with us in prayer, on television, radio and the internet.

This afternoon, Holy Father, as we were preparing for your arrival, we reflected prayerfully on how the Catholic Church plays its part in harnessing the spirit of humble and loving service through the work of its agencies and charities at home and abroad. As a Catholic community we know that authentic Christian life must be grounded in a daily spiritual encounter with the living God, and in fulfilling the command of Jesus Christ, 'Love one another as I have loved you.'

We have come from all over Britain to share this historic moment with you, and to celebrate and rejoice in the truth that God loves every human being unconditionally; irrespective of race, colour or creed. With you this evening we witness to the joy of being a follower of Jesus Christ, the light of the world, who stands at the door of every heart patiently waiting to be let in.

Holy Father, where we stand has a profound historical significance. Over 400 years ago Catholic and Anglican martyrs witnessed to their faith in Jesus Christ, when they were put to death at Tyburn, a short distance from here. We give thanks to God that in more recent times, the Christian Churches in our land work together in the light of the Gospel for the common good of all in this country.

There is so much that unites us and we are committed to continuing the search for that visible unity for which Christ prayed.

During our liturgy this evening, on the eve of the Beatification of John Henry, Cardinal Newman, we will spend time in Christ's presence, meditating on the scriptures and on Cardinal Newman's life and words. We pray that our hearts will be ever more open to the presence and power of the Holy Spirit, so that our lives may radiate the Light of Christ to those around us.

Finally, Holy Father, we assure you of our love, our support and our prayers; for your ministry as Chief Shepherd of the Church; for coming to confirm us in the faith; and especially for teaching us by your own example what it means to be steadfast in our fidelity to the person and teaching of Jesus Christ. Thank you, Holy Father, for being with us this evening and for leading us now in this Vigil of Prayer.

Pope Benedict greets Archbishop Peter Smith at the start of the Prayer Vigil

THE ADDRESS OF THE HOLY FATHER

His Holiness Pope Benedict XVI's Address during the Vigil in Hyde Park

8:30 pm Saturday 18 September 2010

My Brothers and Sisters in Christ,

This is an evening of joy, of immense spiritual joy, for all of us. We are gathered here in prayerful vigil to prepare for tomorrow's Mass, during which a great son of this nation, John Henry, Cardinal Newman will be declared Blessed. How many people, in England and throughout the world, have longed for this moment! It is also a great joy for me, personally, to share this experience with you. As you know, Newman has long been an important influence in my own life and thought, as he has been for so many people beyond these isles. The drama of Newman's life invites us to examine our lives, to see them against the vast horizon of God's plan, and to grow in communion with the Church of every time and place: the Church of the apostles, the Church of the martyrs, the Church of the saints, the Church which Newman loved and to whose mission he devoted his entire life.

I thank Archbishop Peter Smith, for his kind words of welcome in your name, and I am especially pleased to see the many young people who are present for this Vigil. This evening, in the context of our common prayer, I would like to reflect with you about a few aspects of Newman's life, which I consider very relevant to our lives as believers and to the life of the Church today.

Let me begin by recalling that Newman, by his own account, traced the course of his whole life back to a powerful experience of conversion which he had as a young man. It was an immediate experience of the truth of God's word, of the objective reality of Christian revelation as handed down in the Church. This experience, at once religious and intellectual, would inspire his vocation to be a minister of the Gospel, his discernment of

A panoramic view of the 80,000 pilgrims in Hyde Park

the source of authoritative teaching in the Church of God, and his zeal for the renewal of ecclesial life in fidelity to the apostolic tradition. At the end of his life, Newman would describe his life's work as a struggle against the growing tendency to view religion as a purely private and subjective matter, a question of personal opinion. Here is the first lesson we can learn from his life: in our day, when an intellectual and moral relativism threatens to sap the very foundations of our society, Newman reminds us that, as men and women made in the image and likeness of God, we were created to know the truth, to find in that truth our ultimate freedom and the fulfilment of our deepest human aspirations. In a word, we are meant to know Christ, who is himself 'the way, and the truth, and the life' (Jn 14:6).

Newman's life also teaches us that passion for the truth, intellectual honesty and genuine conversion are costly. The truth that sets us free cannot be kept to ourselves; it calls for testimony, it begs to be heard, and in the end its convincing power comes from itself and not from the human eloquence or arguments in which it may be couched. Not

far from here, at Tyburn, great numbers of our brothers and sisters died for the faith; the witness of their fidelity to the end was ever more powerful than the inspired words that so many of them spoke before surrendering everything to the Lord. In our own time, the price to be paid for fidelity to the Gospel is no longer being hanged, drawn and quartered, but it often involves being dismissed out of hand, ridiculed or parodied. And yet, the Church cannot withdraw from the task of proclaiming Christ and his Gospel as saving truth, the source of our ultimate happiness as individuals and as the foundation of a just and humane society.

Finally, Newman teaches us that if we have accepted the truth of Christ and committed our lives to him, there can be no separation between what we believe and the way we live our lives. Our every thought, word and action must be directed to the glory of God and the spread of his Kingdom. Newman understood this, and was the great champion of the prophetic office of the Christian laity. He saw clearly that we do not so much accept the truth in a purely intellectual act, as embrace it in a spiritual dynamic that penetrates to the core of our being. Truth is passed on not merely

149

by formal teaching, important as that is, but also by the witness of lives lived in integrity, fidelity and holiness; those who live in and by the truth instinctively recognise what is false and, precisely as false, inimical to the beauty and goodness which accompany the splendour of truth, *veritatis splendor*.

Tonight's first reading is the magnificent prayer in which Saint Paul asks that we be granted to know 'the love of Christ which surpasses all understanding' (Eph 3:14-21). The Apostle prays that Christ may dwell in our hearts through faith (cf. Eph 3:17) and that we may come to 'grasp, with all the saints, the breadth and the length, the height and the depth' of that love. Through faith we come to see God's word as a lamp for our steps and light for our path (cf. Ps 119:105). Newman, like the countless saints who preceded him along the path of Christian discipleship, taught that the 'kindly light' of faith leads us to realise the truth about ourselves, our dignity as God's children, and the sublime destiny which

Benediction by the Holy Father in Hyde Park

awaits us in heaven. By letting the light of faith shine in our hearts, and by abiding in that light, through our daily union with the Lord in prayer and participation in the life-giving sacraments of the Church, we ourselves become a light to those around us; we exercise our 'prophetic office'; often, without even knowing it, we draw people one step closer to the Lord and his truth. Without the life of prayer, without the interior transformation which takes place through the grace of the sacraments,

we cannot, in Newman's words, 'radiate Christ'; we become just another 'clashing cymbal' (1 Cor 13:1) in a world filled with growing noise and confusion, filled with false paths leading only to heartbreak and illusion.

One of the Cardinal's best-loved meditations includes the words, 'God has created me to do him some definite service. He has committed some work to me which he has not committed to another' (*Meditations on Christian Doctrine*). Here we see Newman's fine Christian realism, the point at which faith and life inevitably intersect. Faith is meant to bear fruit in the transformation of our world through the power of the Holy Spirit at work in the lives and activity of believers. No one who looks realistically at our world today could think that Christians can afford to go on with business as usual, ignoring the profound crisis of faith which has overtaken our society, or simply trusting that the patrimony of values handed down by the Christian centuries will continue to inspire and shape the future of our society. We know that in times of crisis and upheaval God has raised up great saints and prophets for the renewal of the Church and Christian society; we trust in his providence and we pray for his continued guidance. But each of us, in accordance with his or her state of life, is called to work for the advancement of God's Kingdom, by imbuing temporal life with the values of the Gospel. Each of us has a mission, each of us is called to change the world, to work for a culture of life, a culture forged by love and respect for the

dignity of each human person. As our Lord tells us in the Gospel we have just heard, our light must shine in the sight of all, so that, seeing our good works, they may give praise to our heavenly Father (cf. Mt 5:16).

Here, I wish to say a special word to the many young people present. Dear young friends: only Jesus knows what 'definite service' he has in mind for you. Be open to his voice resounding in the depths of your heart: even now his heart is speaking to your heart. Christ has need of families to remind the world of the dignity of human love and the beauty of family life. He needs men and women who devote their lives to the noble task of education, tending the young and forming them in the ways of the Gospel. He needs those who will consecrate their lives to the pursuit of perfect charity, following him in chastity, poverty and obedience, and serving him in the least of our brothers and sisters. He needs the powerful love of contemplative religious, who sustain the Church's witness and activity through their constant prayer. And he needs priests, good and holy priests, men who are willing to lay down their lives for their sheep. Ask our Lord what he has in mind for you! Ask him for the generosity to say 'Yes!' Do not be afraid to give yourself totally to Jesus. He will give you the grace you need to fulfil your vocation. Let me finish these few words by warmly inviting you to join me next year in Madrid for 'World Youth Day'. It is always a wonderful occasion to grow in love for Christ and to be encouraged in a joyful life of faith along with thousands of other young people. I hope to see many of you there!

And now, dear friends, let us continue our vigil of prayer by preparing to encounter Christ, present among us in the Blessed Sacrament of the Altar. Together, in the silence of our common adoration, let us open our minds and hearts to his presence, his love, and the convincing power of his truth. In a special way, let us thank him for the enduring witness to that truth offered by Cardinal John Henry Newman. Trusting in his prayers, let us ask the Lord to illumine our path, and the path of all British society, with the kindly light of his truth, his love and his peace. Amen.

Christ has need of families to remind the world of the dignity of human love and the beauty of family life. He needs men and women who devote their lives to the noble task of education, tending the young and forming them in the ways of the Gospel.

- Pope Benedict XVI

Faces in the crowds, and a baby lifted up for the Holy Father to kiss

LEAD KINDLY LIGHT

Lead, Kindly Light, amid the encircling gloom
　　Lead Thou me on!
The night is dark, and I am far from home –
　　Lead Thou me on!
Keep Thou my feet; I do not ask to see
The distant scene - one step enough for me.

I was not ever thus, nor pray'd that Thou
　　Shouldst lead me on.
I loved to choose and see my path, but now
　　Lead Thou me on!
I loved the garish day, and, spite of fears,
Pride ruled my will: remember not past years.

So long Thy power hath blest me, sure it still
　　Will lead me on,
O'er moor and fen, o'er crag and torrent, till
　　The night is gone;
And with the morn those angel faces smile
Which I have loved long since, and lost awhile.

THE NEW ENGLISH ORCHESTRA

The New English Orchestra was founded by Nigel Swinford, its Artistic Director and Conductor, in 1976. It was born out of his vision of a company of Christian believers proficient in music, but who put Christ first in their lives, coming together for special musical projects.

The New English Orchestra's members are working professionals, but when they perform together their emphasis is on worship and in shedding a specifically Christian light on a broad range of music. The main bulk of their work for the last 35 years has been to make a spiritual contribution to the Salzburg Music Festival, with countless performances in the great Cathedral there and in the Benedictine Monastery of St Peter's, the birthplace of Christianity in that part of Europe.

All the members of the New English Orchestra are Christians drawn from different traditions and there is a strong emphasis on ecumenism in their work. Indeed, the Salzburger Festmesse was composed by conductor Nigel Swinford with the specific purpose of bringing Christians of all traditions together in worship. It was first performed at Klagenfurt Cathedral in 1981, but then again at the 10 am Mass on the opening Sunday of the 1987 Salzburg Festival.

Pope Benedict, a musician himself, thanks Musical Director Nigel Swinford

The Orchestra has, of course, played many times in England, including appearances on the BBC, at the National Exhibition Centre and the Royal Albert Hall. In past years it has also visited Sweden, Russia, Spain and Switzerland. The New English Orchestra has also for many years performed Prayer Vigils in cathedrals up and down the land. Its most recent Vigil took place in November 2009 at Canterbury Cathedral.

Over the last four years, the Orchestra has been regularly performing in Rome, devising ground-breaking spatial effects in the Pantheon, whilst enjoying the privilege of sharing the Gospel via its highly popular 'Recreatio' events, which combine music and scripture readings in a 45-minute presentation, for the benefit of the thousands of tourists who come to explore the city's wonderful buildings.

The Orchestra has also played in Santa Maria Sopra Minerva, titular church of Cardinal Murphy-O'Connor, and in the beautiful church of San Giovanni in Laterano - the Pope's church, in his capacity as Bishop of Rome. During such visits they were often invited by Her Britannic Majesty's Ambassador to the Holy See, His Excellency Mr Francis Campbell, to perform small chamber concerts in his residence for his special guests. This led to a meeting with Father Andrew Headon, then Vice-Rector of the Venerable English College, who invited them to celebrate the opening of the newly refurbished College Chapel, in October 2009.

Father Andrew kindly contacted the New English Orchestra again earlier this year, when plans for the Papal Visit to the United Kingdom were put in place and he had been entrusted with the role of co-ordinating the Hyde Park Vigil. So the New English Orchestra is especially delighted to have been able to accept his invitation to provide the core music for this large event, presided over by Pope Benedict XVI.

Nigel Swinford is the Artistic Director and Founder of the New English Orchestra and Singers, and Director of Music for the Vigil in Hyde Park.

A REFLECTION

Nigel Swinford, Artistic Director and Founder of the New English Orchestra and Singers

A Reflection as Director of Music for the Vigil

It's pretty lonely being a Musical Director on Hyde Park stage with 80,000 pilgrims behind you, innumerable Bishops and Cardinals banked to your left, a large choir and orchestra spread out in front of you, whilst His Holiness the Pope conducts those awesome silent moments in the Liturgy. What if your ear piece falls out and you don't know what music you should be starting next, or when? It's the stuff of nightmares.

The day had started well; inside the hospitality tent were all my friends from the New English Orchestra. The musical trio 'The Priests' were there, ready to sing three numbers that we were to accompany; new friends too from all over the country, who had come to sing in this Prayer Vigil. We had hardly any time to rehearse properly, but they seemed to be there with their hearts open to hear the beating of His heart, as Newman had suggested.

Now we were on stage and nothing could have prepared us for the sight of tens of thousands of people there for the Prayer Vigil. I heard a voice in my (secure) ear piece say, 'Save us Lord our God - GO NIGEL!' I brought my arm down and off we went with Christopher Walker's stirring setting from Psalm 106.

And so the praise unfolded: African music, Gospel, excerpts from Handel's Messiah, stirring modern hymns like John Foley's 'One Bread, One Body', Bernadette Farrell's 'Christ be our light', Graham Kendrick's 'Shine Jesus Shine', the words of this last so utterly similar to Newman's prayer on radiance which came in the ensuing Liturgy.

The Popemobile arrived, the noise levels rose, the whooping excitement was almost palpable. One of the Singers said to me afterwards, 'He has come and told this nation exactly what it needs to hear!' At one stage he turned to the young people specifically, he advised them to come to the Lord and ask what He wanted for them in their future lives.

We worshipped again - *Adoramus te Domine*, with even the Orchestra improvising, offering their very instruments to the Lord. We sang the words of God. 'Be still and know that I am God. I am the Lord that healeth thee'. Could anything get better?

Then we sang the final hymn. I noticed a security man moving towards me. I was gently but firmly led towards the front of the stage, directly into the path of the oncoming Pope! He was beaming and I found myself looking into the eyes of a gentle, friendly man who, for that moment, even though we were surrounded by 80,000 others, was paying me full attention. He seemed in no hurry, and proceeded to express his congratulations and appreciation for our worship-leading. 'It is a great privilege to meet you', I said. 'God bless you.' We shook hands and then he was gone.

We sang John Rutter's 'The Lord bless you and keep you' and then we looked straight at Jesus Himself. We sang and played 'Worthy is the Lamb that was slain and hath redeemed us to God by His blood, to receive power and riches, and wisdom, and strength and honour and glory and blessing. Amen'.

REFLECTIONS FROM YOUNG PEOPLE

Miriam Furze, a-23-year old Christian from London, a singer with the 'New English Orchestra and Singers' at the Prayer Vigil

I love singing the Hallelujah Chorus. Granted, it is one of the most over-played pieces of choral music of all time, but if you listen to the words, really listen, it is also one of the most powerful proclamations of truth that there is. It is not often that you get the opportunity to proclaim the truth that Jesus Christ is 'King of Kings and Lord of Lords' together with 80,000 other people gathered in the middle of London, at the centre of Hyde Park.

From the music of Taizé, to the prayer of Cardinal Newman, the Hyde Park Vigil revolved around the theme of light; God's light which transforms us, and which, shining through us makes us a light to others. 'You are the light of the world. A city built on a hill-top cannot be hidden … in the same way your light must shine in the sight of men'. Hundreds of candles were lit in the darkness to symbolise the words that had been spoken; and to be taken back to each parish to 'shine in the sight of men' in every corner of the country.

Just as the light of the Church is meant to be seen, so too the truth of Christ's Lordship is meant to be heard. As Pope Benedict said, 'We were created to know [this] truth, to find in [it] our ultimate freedom and the fulfilment of our deepest human aspirations…[This] truth that sets us free cannot be kept to ourselves; it calls for testimony, it begs to be heard'. On Saturday it certainly was, and that is worth a 'Hallelujah!'

Rebecca Binney, a 22-year-old Catholic who has attended World Youth Days, went to the Vigil with her family

The Hyde Park Vigil made you realise that you were part of a wonderful vibrant and open family. Emotional reunions heightened the sense of happy expectation in the mass of friendly faces. People from all walks of life awaited the Holy Father, as a single gold heart balloon drifted up to the sun.

The procession of banners revealed the true depth and role of Catholicism in England today. The line was long and diverse - it brought tears to your eyes to see the effort that everyone puts into living out their belief in the sacred value of each human being.

The arrival of the Holy Father caused a hush to fall and calmness seemed to descend as we all focused on the small white light of the Popemobile in the gathering darkness. The face of Pope Benedict spread peace throughout my being, as he waved his hands in an all-inclusive blessing that washed over the crowd, in waves of love.

Pope Benedict spoke to us all of Newman's witness and living in the light of truth. We all stood listening in a disruption to our daily routine that appeared like a wonderful moral and spiritual boost; sent to prepare us for an inspired return into secular society with our own unique God-given mission.

At Adoration, the altar was covered in stars like another night sky and the figure of our Supreme Pontiff stood like the most beautiful moonbeam, with the Eucharist held aloft as the greatest treasure.

As one crowd, we kneeled and stood at the instigation of our Holy Father and it felt truly as though we were all one heart, in that field with no roof: one body of worship and a witness to the world around us, of the great power of love in our faith.

Archbishop Bernard Longley and his team from the Archdiocese of Birmingham shown round Cofton Park by WRG

The Papal MC, Mgr Guido Marini and Papal Visit Organiser Mgr Andrew Summersgill (second and third left) visit Cofton Park on 7 July 2010

Archbishop Bernard Longley before the Mass of Beatification with Father Timothy Menezes,
Local Coordinator for Liturgy (centre) and Father Richard Duffield, Provost of the Birmingham Oratory.

The ever-helpful Lizzie Pocock, Production Assistant, WRG Creative Communications Ltd, showing Canon Patrick Browne (far right)
Local Coordinator for the Papal Visit to the Archdiocese of Birmingham, the planned layout of Cofton Park.

THE MASS OF BEATIFICATION OF THE VENERABLE JOHN HENRY NEWMAN

The Most Reverend Bernard Longley Archbishop of Birmingham - Welcome Address to His Holiness Pope Benedict XVI

Cofton Park, Birmingham
10:25 am Sunday 19 September 2010

Most Holy Father,

It is with great joy that I welcome you here to Birmingham on the final morning of your visit. Over recent days, you have been among us as a pilgrim sharing your own search for the truth and goodness of God. As our Supreme Pastor, you have led us closer to Jesus Christ to be refreshed from the 'well-springs of the Trinity'.

In following your Apostolic Journey we have seen you reach out and touch the hearts and minds of many, within our countries and beyond, by being in our midst and by making us more aware of the presence of Christ the Good Shepherd. As the Successor of Saint Peter, you have encouraged us to draw closer to the rock upon which the Church is built and to recognise it as the true source of living water that can quench our thirst.

Now, Holy Father, we are united with you in prayer in this city which was the chosen and adopted home of the Venerable John Henry Newman. We gather close to the place where his earthly remains were laid to rest and in these hills where he would often come for refreshment and peace. In this place, we thank you for presenting him to us anew – a sure well-spring of goodness and truth where we may find refreshment and strength for our own pilgrimage of faith.

As we come to celebrate his Beatification with you today, we give thanks to God for all those whose influence brought blessings to Cardinal Newman - especially for those who had nurtured his faith within the Church of England and for Blessed Dominic of the Mother of God who first ministered to him sacramentally within the Catholic Church.

We ask you, Holy Father, to draw us again into the eucharistic presence of the Lord, so that we may soon acclaim the Venerable John Henry Newman among the Blessed.

More than 50,000 pilgrims welcome Pope Benedict to Cofton Park

The face of the new Beatus is unveiled electronically — a first

THE DECLARATION OF BEATIFICATION

The Rite of Beatification
The Most Reverend Bernard Longley,
Archbishop of Birmingham requested
that the Venerable John Henry Cardinal
Newman be Beatified

Cofton Park, Birmingham
10:35 am Sunday 19 September 2010

The Vice-Postulator of the Cause, Father Richard Duffield, Provost of the Oratory in Birmingham, read a short biography of Cardinal Newman.

His Holiness Pope Benedict XVI

According to the request of our Brother Bernard Longley, Archbishop of Birmingham, of many other Brothers in the episcopate, and many of the faithful, after consultation with the Congregation for the Causes of Saints, by our apostolic authority we declare that the Venerable Servant of God John Henry, Cardinal Newman, priest of the Congregation of the Oratory, shall henceforth be invoked as Blessed and that his feast shall be celebrated every year on the ninth of October, in the places and according to the norms established by Church law. In the name of the Father, and of the Son, and of the Holy Spirit.

Everyone present responded - Amen.

The portrait of the new Blessed was unveiled electronically (a first) and his relics placed beside the altar.

THE HOMILY OF THE HOLY FATHER

His Holiness Pope Benedict XVI's Homily given during the Beatification Mass

Cofton Park, Birmingham
11:15 am Sunday 19 September 2010

Dear Brothers and Sisters in Christ,

This day that has brought us together here in Birmingham is a most auspicious one. In the first place, it is the Lord's day, Sunday, the day when our Lord Jesus Christ rose from the dead and changed the course of human history for ever, offering new life and hope to all who live in darkness and in the shadow of death. That is why Christians all over the world come together on this day to give praise and thanks to God for the great marvels he has worked for us. This particular Sunday also marks a significant moment in the life of the British nation, as it is the day chosen to commemorate the seventieth anniversary of the Battle of Britain. For me, as one who lived and suffered through the dark days of the Nazi regime in Germany, it is deeply moving to be here with you on this occasion, and to recall how many of your fellow citizens sacrificed their lives, courageously resisting the forces of that evil ideology. My thoughts go in particular to nearby Coventry, which suffered such heavy bombardment and massive loss of life in November 1940. Seventy years later, we recall with shame and horror the dreadful toll of death and destruction that war brings in its wake, and we renew our resolve to work for peace and reconciliation wherever the threat of conflict looms. Yet there is another, more joyful reason why this is an auspicious day for Great Britain, for the Midlands, for Birmingham. It is the day that sees Cardinal John Henry Newman formally raised to the altars and declared Blessed.

I thank Archbishop Bernard Longley for his gracious welcome at the start of Mass this morning. I pay tribute to all who have worked so hard over many years to promote the cause of Cardinal Newman, including the Fathers of the Birmingham Oratory and the members of the Spiritual Family *Das Werk*. And I greet everyone here from Great Britain, Ireland, and further afield; I thank you for your presence at this celebration, in which we give glory and praise to God for the heroic virtue of a saintly Englishman.

England has a long tradition of martyr saints, whose courageous witness has sustained and inspired the Catholic community here for centuries. Yet it is right and fitting that we should recognise today the holiness of a confessor, a son of this nation who, while not called to shed his blood for the Lord, nevertheless bore eloquent witness to him in the course of a long life devoted to the

Sr Mary Dechant and Mother Catherine Strolz of the Spiritual Family 'Das Werk'

priestly ministry, and especially to preaching, teaching, and writing. He is worthy to take his place in a long line of saints and scholars from these islands, Saint Bede, Saint Hilda, Saint Aelred, Blessed Duns Scotus, to name but a few. In Blessed John Henry, that tradition of gentle scholarship, deep human wisdom and profound love for the Lord has borne rich fruit, as a sign of the abiding presence of the Holy Spirit deep within the heart of God's people, bringing forth abundant gifts of holiness.

Cardinal Newman's motto, '*Cor ad cor loquitur*', or 'Heart speaks unto heart', gives us an insight into his understanding of the Christian life as a call to holiness, experienced as the profound desire of the human heart to enter into intimate communion with the Heart of God. He reminds us that faithfulness to prayer gradually transforms us into the divine likeness. As he wrote in one of his many fine sermons, 'a habit of prayer, the practice of turning to God and the unseen world in every season, in every place, in every emergency – prayer, I say, has what may be called a natural effect in spiritualising and elevating the soul. A man is no longer what he was before; gradually

... he has imbibed a new set of ideas, and become imbued with fresh principles' (Parochial and Plain Sermons, iv, 230-231). Today's Gospel tells us that no one can be the servant of two masters (cf. Lk 16:13), and Blessed John Henry's teaching on prayer explains how the faithful Christian is definitively taken into the service of the one true Master, who alone has a claim to our unconditional devotion (cf. Mt 23:10). Newman helps us to understand what this means for our daily lives: he tells us that our divine Master has assigned a specific task to each one of us, a 'definite service', committed uniquely to every single person: 'I have my mission', he wrote, 'I am a link in a chain, a bond of connexion between persons. He has not created me for naught. I shall do good, I shall do his work; I shall be an angel of peace, a preacher of truth in my own place ... if I do but keep his commandments and serve him in my calling' (Meditations and Devotions, 301-2).

The definite service to which Blessed John Henry was called involved applying his keen intellect and his prolific pen to many of the most pressing 'subjects of the day'. His insights into the relationship between faith and reason, into the

all over the world. I would like to pay particular tribute to his vision for education, which has done so much to shape the ethos that is the driving force behind Catholic schools and colleges today. Firmly opposed to any reductive or utilitarian approach, he sought to achieve an educational environment in which intellectual training, moral discipline and religious commitment would come together. The project to found a Catholic University in Ireland provided him with an opportunity to develop his ideas on the subject, and the collection of discourses that he published as 'The Idea of a University' holds up an ideal from which all those engaged in academic formation can continue to learn. And indeed, what better goal could teachers of religion set themselves than Blessed John Henry's famous appeal for an intelligent, well-instructed laity: 'I want a laity, not arrogant, not rash in speech, not disputatious, but men who know their religion, who enter into it, who know just where they stand, who know what they hold and what they do not, who know their creed so well that they can give an account of it, who know so much of history that they can defend it' (The Present Position of Catholics in England, ix, 390). On this day when the author of those words is raised to the altars, I pray that, through his intercession and example,

vital place of revealed religion in civilised society, and into the need for a broadly-based and wide-ranging approach to education were not only of profound importance for Victorian England, but continue today to inspire and enlighten many

Pope Benedict receives Father Gregory Winterton of the Birmingham Oratory, tireless servant of the Newman Cause

all who are engaged in the task of teaching and catechesis will be inspired to greater effort by the vision he so clearly sets before us.

While it is John Henry Newman's intellectual legacy that has understandably received most attention in the vast literature devoted to his life and work, I prefer on this occasion to conclude with a brief reflection on his life as a priest, a pastor of souls. The warmth and humanity underlying his appreciation of the pastoral ministry is beautifully expressed in another of his famous sermons: 'Had Angels been your priests, my brethren, they could not have condoled with you, sympathised with you, have had compassion on you, felt tenderly for you, and made allowances for you, as we can; they could not have been your patterns and guides, and have led you on from your old selves into a new life, as they can who come from the midst of you' ('Men, not Angels: the Priests of the Gospel', Discourses to Mixed Congregations, 3). He lived out that profoundly human vision of priestly ministry in his devoted care for the people of Birmingham during the years that he spent at the Oratory he founded, visiting the sick and the poor, comforting the bereaved, caring for those in prison. No wonder

that on his death so many thousands of people lined the local streets as his body was taken to its place of burial not half a mile from here. One hundred and twenty years later, great crowds have assembled once again to rejoice in the Church's solemn recognition of the outstanding holiness of this much-loved father of souls. What better way to express the joy of this moment than by turning to our heavenly Father in heartfelt thanksgiving, praying in the words that Blessed John Henry Newman placed on the lips of the choirs of angels in heaven:

> *Praise to the Holiest in the height*
> *And in the depth be praise;*
> *In all his words most wonderful,*
> *Most sure in all his ways!*
> *(The Dream of Gerontius)*

The Recitation of the Angelus Domini

Cofton Park, Birmingham
12:00 pm Sunday 19 September 2010

Brothers and Sisters in Jesus Christ,

I am pleased to send my greetings to the people of Seville where, just yesterday, Madre María de la Purísima de la Cruz was Beatified. May Blessed María be an inspiration to young women to follow her example of single-minded love of God and neighbour.

When Blessed John Henry Newman came to live in Birmingham, he gave the name 'Maryvale' to his first home here. The Oratory that he founded is dedicated to the Immaculate Conception of the Blessed Virgin and the Catholic University of Ireland he placed under the patronage of Mary, *Sedes Sapientiae*. In so many ways, he lived his priestly ministry in a spirit of filial devotion to the Mother of God. Meditating upon her role in the unfolding of God's plan for our salvation, he was moved to exclaim: 'Who can estimate the holiness and perfection of her, who was chosen to be the Mother of Christ? What must have been her gifts, who was chosen to be the only near earthly relative of the Son of God, the only one whom He was bound by nature to revere and look up to; the one appointed to train and educate Him, to instruct Him day by day, as He grew in wisdom and in

A drawing of Cardinal Newman at Rednal during 1881

stature?' (Parochial and Plain Sermons, ii, 131-2). It is on account of those abundant gifts of grace that we honour her, and it is on account of that intimacy with her divine Son, that we naturally seek her intercession for our own needs and the needs of the whole world. In the words of the Angelus, we turn now to our Blessed Mother and commend to her the intentions that we hold in our hearts.

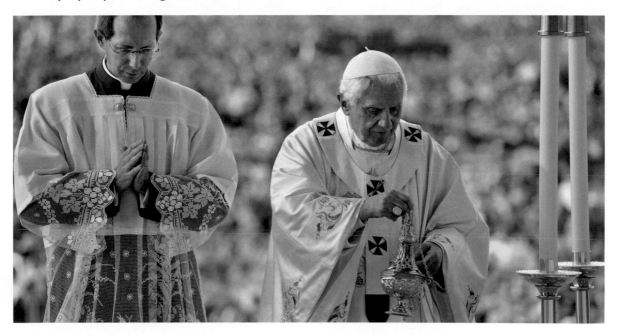

Joyful crowds celebrate with the Holy Father at Cofton Park, Birmingham

Moments of thoughtful prayer during the Beatification ceremony at Cofton Park, Birmingham

REFLECTIONS ON THE BEATIFICATION OF BLESSED JOHN HENRY NEWMAN

Deacon Jack Sullivan, from Marshfield, Massachusetts

A Reflection on the Beatification of Blessed John Henry Newman written following the Beatification Mass in Cofton Park

Cardinal Newman often expressed the view that divine providence guided his steps in his quest for that kindly light of truth. A journey towards sublime truth, but often marked by obstacles and trials. When immersed in darkness he often longed for the light which would mark his steps, as he travelled on the path marked out for him. Cardinal Newman was denied the view he longed for, a view of that distant scene, but one step on this path was enough for him.

Indeed, struggles merely add to one's desire to embrace that quick glimpse of the ultimate beauty of God as we travel toward it. Trials and struggles cause us to exercise our faith and trust in God's benevolent providence. By its practice, we indeed advance one step at a time. Cardinal Newman would say that we cannot embrace the beautiful side of our faith while casting aside what is severe. It is by persevering through struggles and trials, that which is severe, that we ultimately attain that which is beautiful.

Nine years ago, on 15 August 2001 on our Lady's Feast Day of the Assumption, I prayed to this unique and saintly man that I might be ordained a Deacon of the Church. I prayed that he might intercede with our loving Lord to enable me to serve his Church, the people of God. Cardinal Newman said 'Yes' to me, but with the condition that I travel the same path as he had; a test of my mettle and commitment if you will; an opportunity to grow and mature; an opportunity to test the degree of self-giving that I would need in order to serve his people.

So I was brought low in the pain of my confusion, uncertainty and darkness. My healing at first took the form of stamina; always trusting in God's loving providence. Through excruciating pain I travelled to attain that same ultimate beauty which Newman sought. If by God's grace I was permitted to be ordained a Deacon of the Church, I prayed that I would be a good one.

For nine long years I struggled and hoped to be empowered to see that distant scene, one agonising step at a time; and through the prayers of he who is always with me, I was led to my heart's goal. That distant scene was made vivid for me when I asked the Holy Father for his blessing that I might worthily proclaim Christ's gospel.

The distant scene was made even more vivid when I stood at the lectern during Cardinal Newman's Mass of Beatification and looked out on thousands of England's faithful, as I proclaimed that kindly light of truth. This view, this scene will stay with me always. All of my trials and struggles had prepared me for this moment. I was not nervous at all, but was in fact strengthened and reassured that Cardinal Newman was with me, and his countrymen were with me. All that I had previously endured was capsulated in that one mysterious moment of joy.

Mrs Carol Sullivan

A Reflection on Jack's healing and the Beatification of Cardinal Newman

Little did I know how much my life would change when Jack asked me for my 'OK', the night before the deadline for filing his application to enter the Diaconate Formation Program. Jack threw himself completely into the programme despite the obstacles he encountered. He persevered through many trials, but it was because of these trials that Jack experienced his miraculous recovery leading to Cardinal Newman's Beatification.

Since his Ordination, Jack has immersed himself in his parish and prison ministry, which he loves so much. Our story since my 'OK' to his application can only be described as a unique adventure in life. Something you've read about in a novel, unbelievable, but true. Through it all, we remain very ordinary.

Deacon Jack Sullivan and his wife Carol

The Beatification of Cardinal Newman is the end of a long road that Jack and I have travelled. We have met many wonderful people along the way. Most people have been supportive, but there have still been many sceptics. We can only tell you what happened and let you know that we believe that Cardinal Newman answered Jack's prayers.

Taking part in the Papal Mass was an incredibly moving moment for me. Pope Benedict has honoured Cardinal Newman by presiding personally, at the Mass of Beatification. I look forward in the future to the Canonisation of Cardinal Newman. I know that he is listening to our prayers.

Mr Brian Sullivan, Deacon Jack Sullivan's son

A Reflection on the healing of his father and the Beatification of Cardinal Newman

My father and Cardinal Newman were an integral part of two of the greatest days of my life. Thanks to the miracle bestowed upon my father through the intercession of Cardinal Newman, my Dad was able to continue with his diaconate. As a deacon, Dad performed the marriage ceremony for Lauren and me.

The second major event has to do with the birth of our daughter, Nora Elizabeth. Nora's birth coincided with Mom and Dad's visit to Birmingham last November, 2009, to recount the story of his miracle of healing. When I called to share the news of the birth of their first grandchild, Mom and Dad were at the Birmingham Oratory and had just visited Newman's chapel.

Another meaningful day for all of us was the day that my father baptised Nora and welcomed Nora into the faith that he loves so much. There was so much joy in my father's eyes as he performed the baptism.

That is the same joy that I saw in my Dad's eyes during our recent trip to Birmingham. The Beatification of Cardinal Newman on Sunday 19 September was an important event for me and my family. To be able to share in this day with my father and to share in his love of the Church and Cardinal Newman has been a once-in-a-lifetime opportunity for Lauren, Nora and myself. I know Dad's faith and devotion will continue to be an integral part of our lives.

A REFLECTION

The Very Reverend Canon Patrick Browne, Administrator of the Metropolitan Cathedral of Saint Chad, Birmingham, and Local Co-ordinator for the Papal Visit to the Archdiocese of Birmingham

A Reflection on the Mass of Beatification at Cofton Park

The arrival of the first truck-load of building material at Cofton Park was proof that the Beatification of John Henry Newman was to take place during Mass, on Sunday 19 September 2010. This was the start of the transformation of the park into a place of worship and the focus of the world, as Pope Benedict XVI declared 'Blessed' the 19th-century parish priest and intellectual.

Hundreds of people use the park daily as a place of leisure, relaxation and sport. Many people admire its peace and tranquillity while reflecting on the beauty and mystery of God's creation. Now work was underway to accommodate tens of thousands of pilgrims from near and far.

The world waited!

Long before dawn, the pilgrims came from afar, disembarking from the coaches in good humour, anticipating what was to be a memorable experience. As they entered the park the sight of the sanctuary array in light, beauty and character heightened their enthusiasm.

The pilgrims would wait!

The sight of the Holy Father's helicopter roused them from their slumbers and weariness to cheer, to wave flags and to welcome. The warmth and sincerity of the welcome was overwhelming. The wait was over!

Pope Benedict XVI was here!

As the Holy Father stood before me in his sacristy, I thought of my father and mother, and what they had given me. Later, as I stood on the sanctuary looking across the park at the tens of thousands of pilgrims, I tried to imagine what roads were followed to be here - not just the way to the Pilgrim Points. What Pilgrim Packs opened the doors of Christ for them? What Pilgrim Passports had accompanied them on the faith journey that led them to this place?

We came, we prayed, now the world is waiting!

Cofton Park has been returned to its normal use, the people are strolling through the trees, admiring the beauty of God's creation, the football teams are competing for points and trophies and dog-walkers are stopping for a moment or two. For the residents nearby, life is back to normal. However for them, for all who visit that park, and for us, it will never be the same again.

Pope Benedict XVI was there!

Pope Benedict arrived by helicopter near Cofton Park for the Mass of Beatification

A REFLECTION

Midland Sculptor Tim Tolkien and artist-blacksmith Chris Yeomans with the half made statue

Tim Tolkien, Metal Sculptor

A Reflection on the commission to create a full-size statue of Blessed John Henry Newman to commemorate his Beatification in Cofton Park

I received a phone call at around lunchtime on 13 July from Birmingham City Councillor Peter Douglas Osborn, asking was I still a Catholic. It was unusual for my religion and not my illustrious ancestor (J R R Tolkien) to be of interest when being short-listed for a job. And what a job! To produce a full-size statue of John Henry Cardinal Newman for Cofton Park, Birmingham, in time for the Papal Visit, some two months hence. Was I interested?

Early meetings included advice from the editor of this book, which was helpful in guiding me towards the true metal of my subject. My first thoughts had been the Grand Cardinal (after Millais), crucifix-adorned in robe and cap. I began to discover the hard-working, learned priest of firm conviction who gave up his cardinal's seat in Rome, to stay amongst the sick and poor of his adopted Birmingham.

This was the John Henry Newman that I hoped to portray; the only deference to his cardinalship being the inclusion of his *zucchetto*, designed to be detachable to allow the molten zinc used in the galvanising process to pass through the statue, ensuring long-term corrosion resistance.

Although the short timescale suggested minimal detail, we needed to include enough information to tell Newman's story authentically. Peter Jennings was lucky enough to have his own bound copy of Newman's *Apologia*, first published in seven weekly parts and perhaps the Cardinal's best-known work. We have been able to reproduce this faithfully and set it at his side on a small table. Blessed John Henry Newman is shown seated, reading glasses in hand, as if he has just finished re-appraising his own writings. The chunky 'carved' chair and small circular table are heavily draped, evoking the late Victorian era, and the flowing cassock with precise buttons and cummerbund are all correct in detail and make up the solid yet fluid forms of the sculpture.

All this is constructed from 2 mm steel plate. Each section was plasma cut out, heated on the forge, shaped by hammers and tongs, welded into place and all joints were ground smooth. I usually work metal cold but this was a project that strongly suggested the need for heat and so I enlisted the skills of a long-term colleague and friend, artist-blacksmith Chris Yeomans.

We didn't actually start cutting and shaping steel until 18 August; 31 days before His Holiness was due to visit the Midlands. Somehow we were

> *John Henry Newman is worthy to take his place in a long line of saints and scholars from these islands, Saint Bede, Saint Hilda, Saint Aelred, Blessed Duns Scotus, to name but a few.*
>
> *- Pope Benedict XVI*

Sculptor Tim Tolkien shows the Pope the statue of Blessed John Henry Newman

time, had forged most of the bodice to his cassock, arms, collar and skull cap. Even on the Saturday morning, poor John Henry still had no hair nor had I any idea as to how it should be made. Chris built the temporary plinth and painted everything, and somehow I was inspired, so by 4.30 pm the statue was complete and an hour later loaded and on its way to Birmingham.

The next morning grey skies hung over Cofton Park to welcome Pope Benedict. I stood next to two members of Newman's family who share some of his facial characteristics. They were pleased to see the likeness that I had achieved. Then the Pope walked calmly towards our statue, smiling a broad smile, as if recognising an old friend before turning and grasping my hands.

At some time in the near future the statue will be permanently sited in the park and will serve not only as a memorial to the best-known clergyman and religious thinker of his day, the now-Blessed John Henry Newman, but also to the very special and uplifting day that Pope Benedict XVI spent with us in Birmingham.

able to put in the uninterrupted 10-16 hours a day necessary to complete the commission in such a short space of time, working 630 hours between us in just four weeks. As the sculpture grew, so did the sense of occasion.

About half-way through the project I was contacted by the Catholic Bishops' Conference of England and Wales, who had got to hear of our intention to commemorate Newman with a statue, and they wanted to ensure this was included in Pope Benedict's official schedule. I was asked to fax over copies of the drawings, so that they could go to Rome for approval. Four days later, not only had His Holiness agreed to bless our statue but it was requested that I meet with him also, a great and unexpected honour.

The week prior to the Papal Visit to Birmingham we were working feverishly. There was a distinct and growing possibility, that despite our best endeavours, we might not get it finished in time. I had been struggling with the face, on and off for three weeks, searching for something beyond his exaggerated features. Chris, during the same

THE VISIT TO THE ORATORY OF ST PHILIP NERI, EDGBASTON

The front of the Oratory House, Edgbaston

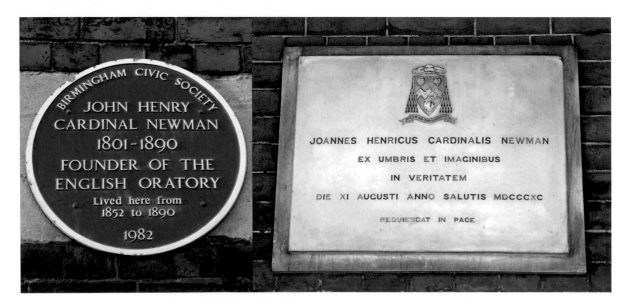

BIRMINGHAM CIVIC SOCIETY

JOHN HENRY
CARDINAL NEWMAN
1801-1890
FOUNDER OF THE
ENGLISH ORATORY
Lived here from
1852 to 1890
1982

JOANNES HENRICUS CARDINALIS NEWMAN

EX UMBRIS ET IMAGINIBUS

IN VERITATEM

DIE XI AUGUSTI ANNO SALUTIS MDCCCXC

REQUIESCAT IN PACE

Mass of Thanksgiving for their Founder at the Birmingham Oratory on Monday 20 September 2010

The Holy Father Pope Benedict XVI signs the visitors' book

The Holy Father is the first pilgrim to pray at the new shrine of Blessed John Henry Newman at the Birmingham Oratory

A REFLECTION

The Reverend Father Gregory Winterton, one-time Actor of the Newman Cause

A Reflection on the Papal Visit and upon the Beatification of the Blessed John Henry Newman

The most striking thing to me about these events, was the way in which what began as a simple object, i.e. promoting the Cause, and which had continued quietly and relentlessly for some thirty-seven years, had suddenly blossomed out into a vast co-operative effort to produce the Mass of Beatification; the happy and joyful visit of the Holy Father to Newman's own house at Edgbaston; and the events in Scotland, London and Birmingham.

These events brought together Oratorian Fathers from all over the world, Newman scholars and devotees likewise, together with Cardinals and Bishops and laity from all five continents.

Newman's motto 'Heart speaks to heart' was verified in a special way and focussed on Blessed John Henry himself as 'A Pastor of Souls', emphasising his gift of friendship, his self-sacrifice and humility and his patient endurance under many trials.

Now, after giving thanks for this weekend and the events following it, we must pray that Blessed John Henry will soon be canonised, and if the Church sees fit, he may then be made a Doctor of the Church.

Pope Benedict clasps the hand of Fr Gregory Winterton outside the Oratory House, Edgbaston

THE HISTORY OF ST MARY'S COLLEGE, OSCOTT

St Mary's College, Oscott where Newman preached his sermon 'The Second Spring'

by Dr Judith Champ

St Mary's College, Oscott, is the seminary of the Catholic Archdiocese of Birmingham, an area which covers the counties of the West Midlands, Staffordshire, Warwickshire, Worcestershire and Oxfordshire. The word 'seminary'

comes from the Latin, 'seminarium', meaning a seedbed, and has been used since the 16th century to describe a college for the formation and training of Catholic priests. Men, who have offered themselves as candidates for priesthood, normally spend six years at Oscott, following a programme of human, spiritual, intellectual and pastoral formation, leading to ordination.

Old Oscott, about two miles from the present college, was the home of Andrew Bromwich, the last seminary priest condemned to death at the time of the Reformation. He had escaped execution in

1679 and when he died in 1702, he left his home for the use of priests who would minister to 'the poor Catholics of the parish of Handsworth'. Throughout the 18th century, a succession of priests lived in Bromwich's house, and in 1794, Oscott College opened there.

In 1803, John Milner became Bishop of the Midland District and under his direction the College was re-launched in August 1808 and dedicated to Saint Mary. By this date, a small but significant milestone had been passed in England's Catholic history. On 21 December 1805, Francis Martyn was ordained. He was the first priest trained wholly in England since the 1560s.

As its numbers outgrew the site, and as Catholics emerged more prominently into national life, Bishop Thomas Walsh, Milner's successor, decided to build a new college on a site overlooking the growing town of Birmingham. It was an ambitious project, and was only made possible through the generosity of wealthy benefactors. The present building, completed in 1838, is a striking landmark built in local red brick and designed to echo elements of an Oxford college.

In the middle decades of the 19th century, Oscott could fairly claim to be the centre of England's Catholic revival. Bishop Walsh brought here the Harvington Library, and, in 1839 he purchased the Marini Library which contained many works of Renaissance scholarship and copies of volumes in the Vatican libraries. The college became associated with leading Catholics, including famous converts to Catholicism. John Henry Newman became a frequent visitor, George Ignatius Spencer, son of the Viscount Althorp, was a benefactor and a member of staff. Nicholas Wiseman was Rector (1840-1847). Already well known in Catholic Europe, he was a man of wide cultural achievements and a prolific author.

Within a few days of his reception into the Catholic Church, Blessed John Henry Newman visited Oscott, where he received the sacrament of Confirmation from Bishop Nicholas Wiseman, on the 1 November 1845. Wiseman welcomed Newman and his companions warmly. Following ordination to the priesthood in Rome in 1847, Newman returned to Birmingham, and on the 1 February 1848, he established the Oratory at Maryvale.

In 1852, Newman was invited to preach at the first Synod of Westminster at Oscott. This gathering, the first of three national synods held at Oscott in the 1850s, marked the formal reinstitution of the Catholic episcopate in England, after the long break since the Reformation.

The story of 'The Second Spring' sermon preached by Newman on the 7 July 1852 became part of the mythology of the Catholic Revival, giving its name to a popular description of what was happening to English Catholicism in the mid 19th century. It was an emotional occasion, with the preacher and most of his hearers in tears at his poignant description of the renewal of Catholic life.

In 2009, a room was set aside for an exhibition of Newman memorabilia from the Oscott collection. It contains portraits, not only of Newman, but of Bishop Wiseman and Bishop Ullathorne, and a copy of the unfinished contemporary painting of the 1852 synod at which Newman preached 'The Second Spring'. The original painting hangs outside the exhibition room on the main staircase.

In the 21st century, Oscott still forms priests and now, permanent deacons. Students are, usually, older on entry, and arrive with several years of experience of employment, or of university; or of both. They bring with them a far greater range of expertise and life experience than did students of earlier generations. Some have come to Christianity as adults. Their courses of study, validated by the Universities of Birmingham and Louvain, are broad-ranging, drawing on the skills of both lay and ordained lecturers.

In 1992, Pope John Paul II issued the teaching document *Pastores Dabo Vobis*, now the inspiration for all seminary formation. The intention of the seminary remains what it has always been – to form men who will 'live the unique and permanent priesthood of Christ' - but: 'It is equally certain that the life and ministry of the priests must also adapt to every era and circumstance of life.'

The Chapel

In 1837, Augustus Welby Pugin, the rising star of Gothic architecture, was brought to Oscott. He was given a free hand in the chapel, creating a glorious visual and spiritual experience for the visitor and worshipper, which would draw them into the mystery of Christianity and closer to God.

Pugin introduced many of the fine arts associated with his revival of medieval gothic design and craftsmanship; memorial brass work, the production of stained glass, silver and gilt plate for use in the liturgy, and encaustic tile-making. The chapel, at the opening of which, in May 1838, he acted as Master of Ceremonies, became a showpiece for his ideas, and attracted national attention.

Dr Judith Champ is an author, historian and Director of Studies at St Mary's College, Oscott

The main entrance of St Mary's College, Oscott

HIS HOLINESS POPE BENEDICT XVI'S MEETING WITH THE BISHOPS OF ENGLAND, SCOTLAND AND WALES IN THE CHAPEL AT OSCOTT HOUSE

His Eminence Keith Patrick, Cardinal O'Brien's Farewell Address to His Holiness Pope Benedict XVI

St Mary's Chapel, Oscott College
5:20 pm Sunday 19 September 2010

Holy Father,

It is a great privilege for me to address you, as Archbishop of St Andrews and Edinburgh and President of the Bishops' Conference of Scotland.

As you prepare to leave us, we remember the joy and pride we felt when we learned of your State visit to the United Kingdom at the invitation of Her Majesty the Queen and Her Majesty's Government.

In Edinburgh, just three days ago, in the Palace of Holyroodhouse, Her Majesty, His Royal Highness, The Prince Philip, Duke of Edinburgh and leaders of Church and State welcomed you and the words you so thoughtfully delivered to us, when you addressed our country.

It was a particular joy for us in Scotland to realise that you would arrive in our country to begin your visit on the 16 of September, the Feast of Saint Ninian. Ninian was of course a bishop, ordained in Rome and sent back to his homeland to spread the Christian message. Your words and your very presence brought to our minds our ancient Christian heritage.

The welcoming cavalcade along Princes Street in Edinburgh reminded a worldwide audience of the Christian roots of our land. Like Saint Ninian before you, you too moved across our countries, strengthening us in that same Christian faith whose seed had been first sown over 1600 years ago.

At Bellahouston Park in Glasgow, the first of your Masses in our country was celebrated with great joy. For many months, our people had been preparing to greet you with very great happiness in prayer and song. Major events followed in England, both temporal and spiritual, allowing you to engage with our fellow Catholics, our Christian brothers and sisters, with civil society, and all people of goodwill.

At the heart of your pilgrimage was the Beatification of John Henry, Cardinal Newman. We are happy to acknowledge the Scottish links of the new Blessed John Henry Newman – coming to Abbotsford in the Scottish Borders for relaxation and prayer and celebrating Mass on the occasions of his visits, wearing the vestments which had been brought to my Chapel in Edinburgh for you to see as a reminder of these Scottish links.

From your first encyclical letter 'Deus Caritas Est', your words have always been given detailed attention and careful study not only by the Catholic faithful but by peoples of all faiths and none.

As the Chief Teacher of our Faith we thank you for the guidance and inspiration you offer us. Your words to us; at Bellahouston Park, Twickenham, Westminster, Hyde Park, at the Beatification, and here in Birmingham will be studied and used to fortify us all in the faith passed on to us through the ages by the apostles and delivered over these four great days by the successor of Peter himself.

Your visit to us was both State and pastoral but our farewell to you is entirely personal. We thank you on behalf of all the people of the United Kingdom for agreeing to spend this time in our midst. On behalf of the bishops and priests gathered here and the whole people of God in our country, I pledge our love and fidelity to you and in asking for your prayers we offer the promise of our own prayers in the certain hope that Almighty God may indeed bless you, Holy Father, and inspire you in your service of love.

This has been a day of great joy for the Catholic community in these islands. Blessed John Henry Newman, as we may now call him, has been raised to the altars as an example of heroic faithfulness to the Gospel and as an intercessor for the Church in this land, that he loved and served so well.
- Pope Benedict XVI

The Pope and Prelates at prayer in the Chapel where Cardinal Newman preached

The Most Reverend Vincent Nichols Archbishop of Westminster's Farewell Address to His Holiness Pope Benedict XVI

St Mary's Chapel, Oscott College
5:30 pm Sunday 19 September 2010

Most Holy Father,

As we gather with you, together with our much loved Apostolic Nuncio, it is my joy and privilege to address you.

After all the joy, excitement and intensity of these four days of your most historic visit, we now cherish these moments of prayerful reflection with you.

This chapel holds a precious place in our history. It was here, in the first gathering of the newly appointed bishops, in 1852, that a new strategy for the Church in these countries was fashioned, a strategy which has proved to be enduring and fruitful. It centred on the importance of education in the faith and on the building up of parish life.

During the Synod, the imagination of the bishops was fired by the powerful preaching of Father John Henry Newman, from that very pulpit. He was

bold enough to speak of a new spring in the history of the Catholic faith in this place.

That historic moment has some resonances for us gathered here today. This moment with you is in a kind of 'Upper Room'. Here, in your guidance and blessing, we seek the inspiration of the Holy Spirit for our mission.

Time and again, you have spoken of the importance of the contribution of the Christian faith in our society, not least because, in your own words, 'if the moral principles underpinning the democratic process are themselves determined by nothing more solid than social consensus, then the fragility of the process becomes all too evident.'(Westminster Hall) We can already sense a new openness to this question, and to the role of faith communities, not only in the stance of the Government but also in the hearts and willingness of so many people. We will pursue and build on these opportunities for the common good of all.

In speaking to us, you have urged young people to find their fulfilment in a love for Christ, a love which will show them that, first, they are loved by Him. That must be true for us too. You have urged our priests to be faithful to their ministry and we bishops to be fathers to our priests. This we will strive to do. You have meditated with us on the 'unity between Christ's sacrifice on the Cross, the Eucharistic sacrifice which he has given to his Church and his eternal priesthood' in which we participate in daily living. Your words point us to our baptismal calling 'to bring the reconciling power of his sacrifice to the world in which we live.'(Westminster Cathedral)

In this context, you have encouraged us in our work of safeguarding and shown an open heart to those who have suffered through our neglect. For this we thank you. You have reminded us of the importance of sensitive care of the elderly, offered with deep respect and recognition of their spiritual journey. You have reached out to our friends in other faiths, committing us again to work with them and seeking from them an open and reciprocal dialogue. You have led us in prayer and dialogue with our fellow brothers and sisters in Christ, strengthening our friendship and co-operation with them. The warmth and depth of our prayer together in Westminster Abbey will long remain in our hearts.

Holy Father, you give us new hearts for the tasks ahead especially in the wonderful gift of declaring John Henry Newman as a blessed model for us to follow. It is an English Parish Priest whom you have beatified and this, for us, is the finest culmination of the Year for Priests. And, as we gather in this College chapel we recognise the importance of the work of fostering vocations and forming men to be the future generations of priests in these countries. This is a work to which we are deeply committed and I know you will give great joy to our seminarians when you greet them this afternoon before leaving.

Holy Father, in this visit you are contributing richly to our history and to the shaping our future. You lift our hearts and reinvigorate us for our ministry especially in the example you give to us with your openness of heart, keenness of mind and gentle eloquence of expression in your unfailing witness to the mystery of Christ.

We take to heart your words that 'we need witnesses of the beauty of holiness, witnesses of the splendour of truth, witnesses of the joy and freedom born of a living relationship with Christ!' (Westminster Cathedral) This is our calling and we renew our dedication to it today.

Your visit to us was both State and pastoral but our farewell to you is entirely personal.

And so, Holy Father, we thank you on behalf of all the people of the United Kingdom for agreeing to spend this time in our midst. On behalf of the bishops and priests and the whole people of God in our country, I pledge our love and prayers for your vital and rich ministry in the Church and in the world. May Almighty God bless you, Holy Father, and inspire you in your service of love.

We also wish to thank you for the gift to this College of the beautiful mosaic of Mary and the child Jesus. It will be treasured.

And I would now ask Archbishop Kelly and Archbishop Smith to come forward to receive from you your gifts for their Provinces.

One of the gifts we wish to present to you is also intensely personal. It concerns the life of 17th century Bartholomew Holzhauser. As you know, Holy Father, Father Holzhauser began his Institute for Secular Clergy in your home- town of Tittmoning, in a building which later became your family home. You speak of this in your own memoires. In the 19th century, interest in Holzhauser revived. He was declared Venerable by your predecessor Leo XIII. This college, St Mary's Oscott, became imbued with the spirit of Holzhauser when the rector, Henry Parkinson (1896-1924) formed this house in that spirit. He played a major role in founding the 'Apostolic Union of Secular Clergy', for the mutual support of priests. He also led the students in a translation of the life of Bartholomew Holzhauser. We have prepared a special edition of that text and we hope that it will remind you that the spirit of Holzhauser is still deeply formative in this house.

Archbishop Vincent Nichols presents the Holy Father with a parting gift

THE ADDRESS OF THE HOLY FATHER AT OSCOTT COLLEGE

The Pontiff addresses the assembled bishops

His Holiness Pope Benedict XVI's Address at Oscott College

St Mary's Chapel, Oscott College
5:40 pm Sunday 19 September 2010

My dear Brother Bishops,

This has been a day of great joy for the Catholic community in these islands. Blessed John Henry Newman, as we may now call him, has been raised to the altars as an example of heroic faithfulness to the Gospel and as an intercessor for the Church in this land, that he loved and served so well. Here in this very chapel in 1852, he gave voice to the new confidence and vitality of the Catholic community in England and Wales after the restoration of the hierarchy, and his words could be applied equally to Scotland a quarter of a century later. His Beatification today is a reminder of the Holy Spirit's continuing action in calling forth gifts of holiness from among the people of Great Britain, so that from east to west and from north to south, a perfect offering of praise and thanksgiving may be made to the glory of God's name.

I thank Cardinal O'Brien and Archbishop Nichols for their words, and in so doing, I am reminded how recently I was able to welcome all of you to Rome for the *Ad Limina* visits of your respective Episcopal Conferences. We spoke then about some of the challenges you face as you lead your people in faith, particularly regarding the urgent need to proclaim the Gospel afresh in a highly secularised environment. In the course of my visit it has become clear to me how deep a thirst there is among the British people for the Good News of Jesus Christ. You have been chosen by God to offer them the living water of the Gospel, encouraging them to place their hopes, not in the vain enticements of this world, but in the firm assurances of the next. As you proclaim the coming of the Kingdom, with its promise of hope for the poor and the needy, the sick and the elderly, the unborn and the neglected, be sure to present in its fullness the life-giving message of the Gospel, including those elements which call into question the widespread assumptions of today's culture. As you know, a Pontifical Council has recently been established for the New Evangelisation of countries of long-standing Christian tradition, and I would encourage you to avail yourselves of its services in addressing the task before you. Moreover, many of the new ecclesial movements have a particular charism for evangelisation, and I know that you will continue to explore appropriate and effective ways of involving them in the mission of the Church.

Since your visit to Rome, political changes in the United Kingdom have focused attention on the consequences of the financial crisis, which has caused so much hardship to countless individuals and families. The spectre of unemployment is casting its shadow over many people's lives, and the long-term cost of the ill-advised investment practices of recent times is becoming all too evident. In these circumstances, there will be additional calls on the characteristic generosity of British Catholics, and I know that you will take a lead in calling for solidarity with those in need. The prophetic voice of Christians has an important role in highlighting the needs of the poor and disadvantaged, who can so easily be overlooked in the allocation of limited resources. In their teaching document *Choosing the Common Good,* the Bishops of England and Wales underlined the importance of the practice of virtue in public life. Today's circumstances provide a good opportunity to reinforce that message, and indeed to encourage people to aspire to higher moral values in every area of their lives, against a background of growing cynicism regarding even the possibility of virtuous living.

Another matter which has received much attention in recent months, and which seriously undermines the moral credibility of Church leaders, is the shameful abuse of children and young people by priests and religious. I have spoken on many occasions of the deep wounds that such behaviour causes, in the victims first and foremost, but also in

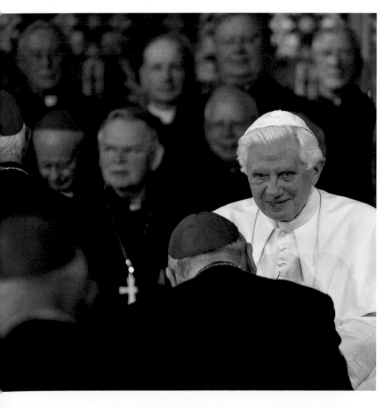

the relationships of trust that should exist between priests and people, between priests and their bishops, and between the Church authorities and the public. I know that you have taken serious steps to remedy this situation, to ensure that children are effectively protected from harm and to deal properly and transparently with allegations as they arise. You have publicly acknowledged your deep regret over what has happened, and the often inadequate ways it was addressed in the past. Your growing awareness of the extent of child abuse in society, its devastating effects, and the need to provide proper victim support should serve as an incentive to share the lessons you have learned with the wider community. Indeed, what better way could there be of making reparation for these sins than by reaching out, in a humble spirit of compassion, towards children who continue to suffer abuse elsewhere? Our duty of care towards the young demands nothing less.

As we reflect on the human frailty that these tragic events so starkly reveal, we are reminded that, if we are to be effective Christian leaders, we must live lives of the utmost integrity, humility and holiness. As Blessed John Henry Newman once wrote, 'O that God would grant the clergy to feel their weakness as sinful men, and the people to sympathise with them and love them and pray for their increase in all good gifts of grace' (Sermon, 22 March 1829). I pray that among the graces of this visit will be a renewed dedication on the part of Christian leaders to the prophetic vocation they have received, and a new appreciation on the part of the people for the great gift of the ordained ministry. Prayer for vocations will then arise spontaneously, and we may be confident that the Lord will respond by sending labourers to bring in the plentiful harvest that he has prepared throughout the United Kingdom (cf. Mt 9:37-38). In this regard, I am glad that I will shortly have the opportunity to meet the seminarians of England, Scotland and Wales, and to assure them of my prayers as they prepare to play their part in bringing in that harvest.

Finally, I should like to speak to you about two specific matters that affect your episcopal ministry at this time. One is the imminent publication of

The Bishops of England, Scotland and Wales grouped round the Bishop of Rome

the new translation of the Roman Missal. I want to take this opportunity to thank all of you for the contribution you have made, with such painstaking care, to the collegial exercise of reviewing and approving the texts. This has provided an immense service to Catholics throughout the English-speaking world. I encourage you now to seize the opportunity that the new translation offers for in-depth catechesis on the Eucharist and renewed devotion in the manner of its celebration. 'The more lively the eucharistic faith of the people of God, the deeper is its sharing in ecclesial life in steadfast commitment to the mission entrusted by Christ to his disciples' (*Sacramentum Caritatis*, 6). The other matter I touched upon in February with the Bishops of England and Wales, when I asked you to be generous in implementing the Apostolic Constitution *Anglicanorum Coetibus*. This should be seen as a prophetic gesture that can contribute positively to the developing relations between Anglicans and Catholics. It helps us to set our sights on the ultimate goal of all ecumenical activity: the restoration of full ecclesial communion in the context of which the mutual exchange of gifts from our respective spiritual patrimonies serves as

an enrichment to us all. Let us continue to pray and work unceasingly in order to hasten the joyful day when that goal can be accomplished.

With these sentiments, I thank you warmly for your hospitality over the past four days. Commending all of you and the people you serve to the intercession of Saint Andrew, Saint David and Saint George, I am pleased to impart my Apostolic Blessing to you and to all the clergy, religious and lay faithful of England, Scotland and Wales.

This has been a day of great joy for the Catholic community in these islands. Blessed John Henry Newman, as we may now call him, has been raised to the altars as an example of heroic faithfulness to the Gospel and as an intercessor for the Church in this land that he loved and served so well.

- Pope Benedict XVI

The Holy Father pictured with seminarians of England, Scotland and Wales in the grounds of of Oscott College

The Holy Father makes a start to leave amid the joy and applause of his hosts

MAY HE SUPPORT US

May he support us all the day long,
till the shades lengthen

and evening comes,

and the busy world is hushed

and the fever of life is over

and our work is done.

Then in his mercy

may he give us a safe lodging

and a holy rest

and peace at the last.

SOME REFLECTIONS

The Right Reverend David McGough
Auxiliary Bishop of Birmingham

A Reflection on the private visit of the Holy Father to St Mary's College, Oscott and the Meeting with the Bishops of England, Scotland and Wales

Pope Benedict's visit to the United Kingdom concluded at Oscott College in Birmingham. Here the Holy Father met with the Bishops of England and Wales and Scotland and greeted students preparing for the priesthood.

For me, this was the most deeply personal moment of the Holy Father's visit. While Oscott College does not figure prominently in the consciousness of the wider Catholic population, it holds a special place in the affection of many parish clergy.

My own experience of the College mirrors that of many priests working throughout the country. It was at Oscott College that we took our first steps towards the priesthood. For many years, as a teacher, Oscott College was the home that I shared with priests and students from Dioceses across the country.

It is difficult to put into words the memories that flooded back, as the Holy Father joined us for lunch in the refectory. So much has been shared at its tables over the generations. Now it was Pope Benedict who sustained our gathering with his wisdom and gentleness.

The chapel at Oscott has nurtured the faith of many generations. Here Cardinal Newman, preaching at the Synod of the newly restored hierarchy in 1852, had spoken of a new 'spring' in the life of the Church. No words can describe the palpable sense of Newman's presence as Pope Benedict XVI, on the very day of Newman's Beatification, addressed the successors of that Synod in the same chapel.

My thoughts also turned to Monsignor H Francis Davis, a much loved professor at Oscott College in the 1950's. For him Newman was a love shared with many students and his writing was instrumental in promoting Newman's Cause. Could he ever have imagined that the Holy Father would come to his beloved Oscott to celebrate the Beatification of John Henry Newman?

The Very Reverend Monsignor Mark Crisp, Rector of St Mary's College, Oscott

A Reflection on the private visit of Pope Benedict XVI to St Mary's College, Oscott

In August, I had the privilege to be in the Holy Land and one of the highlights was standing in the ruined streets of Capernaum, between the synagogue and Saint Peter's house. It is an amazing feeling to know that you are walking in the streets where so many of the events in the life of Jesus took place.

Dr Judith Champ and Mgr Mark Crisp

Dr Judith Champ, Director of Studies and College Historian at St Mary's College, Oscott

A Reflection on The Holy Father's visit to Oscott

For half of my life I have been writing and talking about momentous events in the history of St Mary's College, Oscott, but that hardly prepared me to experience a real moment in history, as we did on Sunday 19 September.

As an historian, I do have a strong sense that Newman and the other great figures in our history are still very much part of the fabric of the College, and that is even more of a reality as a result of the Papal Visit.

Newman was a frequent visitor to Oscott, he was confirmed in the College chapel and preached there on many occasions, including at the synod of 1852. His presence in the College has been truly enlivened by the gathering of the whole family of the Church – the Pope, bishops, priests, religious and lay people at Oscott, with Newman as the focus.

Newman was heard to murmur after the joyous Oscott celebration of his appointment as cardinal in 1879, 'I did not know Oscott was so much in sympathy with me'. That sympathy is even more in evidence now. Oscott cherishes Newman's memory and reveres him as a model of holiness and pastoral care to inspire generations of seminarians. He spoke in 1852 of the 'Second Spring' of the Church in England, as it emerged from the penal times, but also of the trials that would face the Church in the years to come.

The Church is never without difficulties, but perhaps the combination of Blessed John Henry Newman and Pope Benedict XVI will bless Oscott and English Catholics with the inspiration of another spring - a time of renewed willingness, hope and energy with which to carry the Gospel into the life of our nation.

As I walked into the synagogue my mobile phone went off. It was one of the police officers in charge of the search team that would be coming to Oscott in preparation for the visit of Pope Benedict XVI. At that moment I couldn't help being struck by the significance of standing near Saint Peter's house, knowing that three weeks later, his successor would be coming to the house where I live.

The Holy Father was coming to Oscott, of course, because of its historical links with Blessed John Henry Newman. In coming to the seminary, however, the successor of Saint Peter was also re-affirming the vocation of all those here who are discerning their call to the priesthood. For they, just like Peter are responding to the call of the Lord; 'Follow me'.

There was a particularly moving moment as the Holy Father was leaving. Gathered on the lawn were bishops, priests, seminarians, our domestic and grounds staff, security personnel, police and even a police dog. It wasn't just the intense excitement which was palpable; it was the great sense of family. At that moment we experienced something far greater than ourselves; something stretching back through the ages to the crowds gathered in Capernaum around Saint Peter's house.

Dr David Symons, Curator of Antiquities and Numismatics, Birmingham Museum and Art Gallery

A Reflection on the visit to Birmingham of the Holy Father

To mark the Pope's visit to Birmingham, the City Council had a replica made of one of the pieces in the recently-discovered Staffordshire Hoard of Anglo-Saxon gold artefacts, the so-called 'Folded Cross', and presented it to the Holy Father when he celebrated Mass at Cofton Park.

The choice of gift was particularly important to me and my colleagues at the Museum. The hoard was found very near Birmingham, and it produced an incredible response from the people of Birmingham when we first put it on display. It was also significant that the replica was made in Birmingham, in the famous Jewellery Quarter, since jewellery has been made there for more than 200 years.

The gift was especially appropriate for His Holiness, since the 'Folded Cross' was made and used within 100 years of Pope Saint Gregory

I sending Saint Augustine to begin the conversion of the pagan English in 597.

My colleague Deborah Cane and I were lucky enough to take the 'Folded Cross', and the other Christian items from the hoard, to Oscott College so that His Holiness could see them in person. It gave us a great sense of satisfaction to do so, especially since several of the bishops had already told us how pleased the Holy Father was by the gift of the replica cross that morning.

To have the opportunity to talk to the Holy Father in person was simply astounding. Although I am not a Catholic, it was a deeply moving experience and something that I shall remember for as long as I live.

Pope Benedict is presented with a replica of the Folded Cross in the Anglo-Saxon hoard by Councillor Alan Rudge, who oversaw the Papal Visit for Birmingham City Council

The Prime Minster David Cameron says farewell to Pope Benedict XVI at the end of his hugely successful State Visit

Remarks made by the Prime Minster at the Conclusion of the State Visit

6:30 pm Sunday 19 September 2010

Your Holiness Pope Benedict, Your Excellencies, Ladies and Gentlemen.

This ceremony brings to a close an incredibly moving four days for our country.

Your Holiness, on this truly historic first State Visit to Britain you have spoken to a nation of six million Catholics but you have been heard by a nation of more than 60 million citizens and by many millions more all around the world.

For you have offered a message not just to the Catholic Church, but to each and every one of us, of every faith and none.

A challenge to us all to follow our conscience, to ask not what are my entitlements, but what are my responsibilities?

To ask not what we can do for ourselves, but what we can do for others?

Cardinal Newman, who was beatified here in Birmingham this morning, once said that one little deed whether by someone who helps 'to relieve the sick and needy' or someone who 'forgives an enemy' evinces more true faith than could be shown by 'the most fluent religious conversation or the most intimate knowledge of Scripture.'

In his immense contribution to the philosophy of higher education, Cardinal Newman reminded the world of the need for education for life not just for the workplace.

That broader education for life mattered because of the responsibilities of each person in society, obligations and opportunities that came from what Cardinal Newman described as the 'common bond of unity' that we all share.

Your Holiness, this common bond has been an incredibly important part of your message to us.

And it's at the heart of the new culture of social responsibility we want to build in Britain.

People of faith – including our 30,000 faith-based charities – are great architects of that new culture.

For many, faith is a spur to action.

It shapes their beliefs and behaviour; and it gives them a sense of purpose.

Crucially, it is their faith that inspires them to help others.

And we should celebrate that.

Faith is part of the fabric of our country. It always has been and it always will be.

As you, Your Holiness, have said, faith is not a problem for legislators to solve but rather a vital part of our national conversation.

And we are proud of that.

But people do not have to share a religious faith or agree with religion on everything to see the benefit of asking the searching questions that you, Your Holiness, have posed to us about our society and how we treat ourselves and each other.

You have really challenged the whole country to sit up and think, and that can only be a good thing.

Because I believe that we can all share in your message of working for the common good and that we all have a social obligation each other, to our families and our communities.

And, of course, our obligations to each other – and our care for each other – must extend beyond these shores, too.

Your Holiness, in our meeting yesterday and in the discussions with the Papal delegation on Friday, evening, we agreed to develop the co-operation between this country and the Holy See, on the key international issues where we share a common goal.

On winning the argument to get to grips with climate change.

On promoting a multi-faith dialogue and working for peace in our world

On fighting poverty and disease.

I passionately believe that we must continue to help the poorest, even in difficult economic times.

A yawning gap between the rich and the poor will be more dangerous and less secure for all of us.

So this country will keep its promises on aid.

We will work to hold other countries to their keep promises too.

And to make sure that money we spend on aid goes to those who need it most.

And I am delighted that the Holy See will be working so actively with us to do all we can to achieve this.

Your Holiness, your presence here has been a great honour for our country.

Now you are leaving us – and I hope with strong memories.

When you think of our country, think of it as one that not only cherishes faith, but one that is deeply, but quietly, compassionate.

I see it in the incredible response to the floods in Pakistan.

I see it in the spirit of community that drives countless good deeds done for friends and neighbours every day.

And in my own life, I have seen it in the many, many kind messages that I have had as I have cradled a new daughter and said goodbye to a wonderful father.

As we stand here in Birmingham, to bid you farewell, let me return to the words of Cardinal Newman.

The Cardinal is greatly remembered here in Birmingham for his care for its people.

During a cholera outbreak in the city, he worked tirelessly among the poor and sick.

And when he himself died, the poor of the city turned out in their thousands to line the streets.

Inscribed on the pall of his coffin, was his motto 'Heart speaks unto heart'.

That has been the theme of this most special visit.

I hope it is a reflection of the welcome that you have received. It is most definitely a fitting tribute to the words you have spoken and the sentiments that you leave behind.

I wish you and your delegation a safe return to Rome.

And I look forward to ever closer co-operation between the United Kingdom and the Holy See, as we redouble our resolve to work for the common good, both here in Britain and with our partners abroad.

The Right Honourable David Cameron, MP, was appointed Prime Minister and First Lord of the Treasury on 11 May 2010, at the head of the coalition Government. He is Conservative MP for Witney, Oxfordshire.

THE DEPARTURE CEREMONY AT BIRMINGHAM INTERNATIONAL AIRPORT

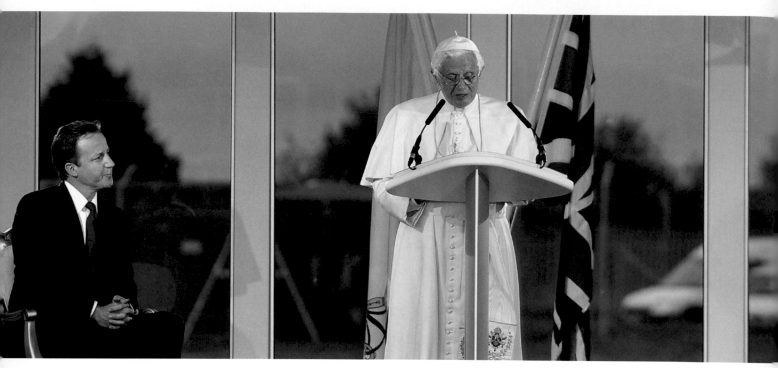

His Holiness Pope Benedict XVI's Farewell Address

Birmingham International Airport
6:45 pm Sunday 19 September 2010

Prime Minister,

Thank you for your kind words of farewell on behalf of Her Majesty's Government and the people of the United Kingdom. I am very grateful for all the hard work of preparation, on the part of both the present and the previous Government, the civil service, local authorities and police, and the many volunteers who patiently helped to prepare for the events of these four days. Thank you for the warmth of your welcome and for the hospitality that I have enjoyed.

During my time with you, I have been able to meet representatives of the many communities, cultures, languages and religions that make up British society. The very diversity of modern Britain is a challenge to its Government and people, but it also represents a great opportunity to further intercultural and interreligious dialogue for the enrichment of the entire community.

In these days, I was grateful for the opportunity to meet Her Majesty The Queen, as well as yourself and other political leaders, and to be able to discuss matters of common interest, both at home and abroad. I was particularly honoured to be invited to address both Houses of Parliament in the historic precincts of Westminster Hall. I sincerely hope that these occasions will contribute to confirming and strengthening the excellent relations between the Holy See and the United Kingdom, especially in co-operation for international development, in care for the natural environment, and in the building of a civil society with a renewed sense of shared values and common purpose.

It was also my pleasure to visit His Grace the Archbishop of Canterbury and the Bishops of the Church of England, and later to pray with them and our fellow Christians in the evocative surroundings of Westminster Abbey, a place which speaks so eloquently of our shared traditions and culture. As Britain is home to so many religious traditions, I was grateful to have the opportunity to meet their representatives and to share some thoughts with them about the contribution that the religions can offer to the development of a healthy pluralistic society.

Naturally, my visit was directed in a special way to the Catholics of the United Kingdom. I treasure the time spent with the bishops, clergy, religious and laity, and with teachers, pupils and older people. It was especially moving to celebrate with them, here in Birmingham, the Beatification of a great son of England, Cardinal John Henry Newman. With his vast legacy of scholarly and spiritual writings, I am certain that he still has much to teach us about Christian living and witness amid the challenges of today's world, challenges which he foresaw with such remarkable clarity.

As I take my leave of you, let me assure you once again of my good wishes and prayers for the peace and prosperity of Great Britain. Thank you very much and God bless you all!

The Pope waves down to the leaving party before entering his aircraft to fly home

"Fly away, Peter!" Silhouetted well-wishers

THE HOLY FATHER REFLECTS ON HIS APOSTOLIC JOURNEY TO THE UNITED KINGDOM

The Address of His Holiness Pope Benedict XVI given during his weekly General Audience

St Peter's Square
Wednesday 22 September 2010

Dear Brothers and Sisters in Christ,

As you know, I have just returned from my first Apostolic Journey to the United Kingdom, and I wish to send my affectionate greetings to all those I met and those who contributed to the visit through the media during four days, which have begun a new and important phase in the long-standing relations between the Holy See and Great Britain.

Last Thursday, I was honoured by the warm welcome of Her Majesty The Queen and the Duke of Edinburgh, in Scotland's historic capital of Edinburgh. Later that day, I celebrated Mass in Glasgow in the presence of many bishops, priests, religious and a great concourse of the faithful against the backdrop of a beautiful sunset at Bellahouston Park, within sight of the place where my beloved predecessor celebrated Mass with the Scots twenty-eight years ago.

Upon arriving in London, I met thousands of Catholic students and schoolchildren at a very joyful celebration, reminding all of us of the excellent and essential work being done by Catholic schools and teachers throughout the land. I then had the pleasure of meeting the clerical and lay representatives of different religions and of discussing the search for the sacred common to all men.

Later, I had the honour of calling upon His Grace the Archbishop of Canterbury who has come on several occasions to meet me in Rome. Our meeting at Lambeth Palace, in the presence of the Bishops of the Church of the England, was very cordial and fraternal. I then crossed the river to Westminster where I was given the unprecedented opportunity to address both Houses of Parliament gathered in Westminster Hall on the importance of a fruitful dialogue between religion and reason, a theme as relevant in the time of Saint Thomas More as it is in our own day. Finally that day, I had the privilege of kneeling in prayer with the Archbishop of Canterbury at the Tomb of Saint Edward in Westminster Abbey, and of giving thanks to God with the Archbishop, the Moderator of the Church of Scotland and other British Christian leaders, for the many blessings God has bestowed upon our efforts to re-knit the fabric of our Christian fellowship.

The next morning, I had the pleasure of greeting Prime Minister David Cameron, Deputy Prime Minister Nick Clegg and Ms Harriet Harman,

Leader of the Opposition, before celebrating Mass in Westminster Cathedral, with a liturgy evocative of the best of the English musical tradition in the celebration of the Roman rite. That afternoon, I was welcomed very cordially by the Little Sisters of the Poor and the elderly people they look after. There I also had the chance to thank and encourage those charged with the safeguarding of children in Britain. That evening I participated at a beautiful Vigil of deep prayerfulness and stillness at Hyde Park, with tens of thousands of the faithful.

On Sunday morning, I travelled to Birmingham where I had the joy of celebrating the Beatification of Cardinal John Henry Newman. Later that day, after a warm and fraternal meeting with all the Bishops of Britain, I was bidden farewell by Prime Minister Cameron during a very cordial speech at Birmingham International Airport on the Government's wish to build a partnership for development with the Catholic Church and others.

Sunday, then, was a moment of deep personal satisfaction, as the Church celebrated the blessedness of a great Englishman, whose life and writings I have admired for many years and who has come to be appreciated by countless people far beyond the shores of his native land. Blessed John Henry Newman's clear-minded search to know and express the truth in charity, at whatever cost to his own personal comfort, status and even friendships, is a wonderful testimony of a pure desire to know and love God in the communion of the Church. His is surely an example that can inspire us all.

Home in Rome, with his own memories of the Visit, and having left millions of memories in British hearts and minds

A REFLECTION

**His Excellency Mr Francis Campbell,
Her Britannic Majesty's Ambassador
to the Holy See**

*A Reflection on the State Visit of His Holiness
Pope Benedict XVI to the United Kingdom*

This was the first official Papal Visit to the United Kingdom. It was styled a Papal Visit with the full status of a State Visit, so as to allow a certain flexibility reflecting the Pope's dual role as a Head of State and also as Head of the Catholic Church.

Pope Benedict's visit was historic. It was so because it was the first time that we were able to honour the Pope with an Official Visit. The relationship with the Holy See is the Crown's oldest diplomatic friendship, dating from 1479, when the Crown first sent an ambassador abroad. John Shirwood was the Crown's first ambassador and he was sent to the Holy See. Throughout the centuries, the relationship between the Holy See and the United Kingdom has survived many challenges, but today it is a key partnership founded on many shared interests in major international issues.

Those shared interests were one of the main reasons why The Queen invited the Pope to visit the United Kingdom in September 2010. That invitation had the full backing of the Prime Minister and his predecessors.

I was able to accompany the Pope during his visit to the United Kingdom; a visit which took him to Edinburgh, Glasgow, London and Birmingham. It is difficult to pick out specific memories when asked to write about such a visit; but there are three points that will remain with me in the coming years when I think of 16-19 September 2010.

The first memory is something that gave me a great deal of satisfaction. It was concerning the number of people who came out to see the Pope

pass by on the street or attend one of the events. As we left Edinburgh Airport, on the morning of 16 September, the Holy Father was greeted by waving crowds who lined the streets of Edinburgh as His Holiness travelled to be received by The Queen at Holyroodhouse. Those early scenes in Edinburgh were repeated later in the day as we travelled to Glasgow along the motorway. Each bridge had crowds of people gathered to see the Pope pass by. As each day went by it was the same – streets lined with people to see the Pope travel down their road. I think the most impressive moment had to be on the evening of 18 September, as the Pope travelled along the Mall leading up to Buckingham Palace. His Holiness was following the traditional route for State Visitors and the Mall was, as is the custom for State Visits, decked with the national flags of the United Kingdom and the Holy See. Over 200,000 people lined the route to see the Holy Father travel to the Prayer Vigil at Hyde Park. Their faces said it all. They represented all walks of life, all ethnicities and races. It was a true reflection of London and it was a welcome like none we had ever seen before on a State Visit.

The second memory was concerning what the Pope said. Pope Benedict's speech at Edinburgh complemented The Queen's as they both spoke about the country's rich Christian heritage. As the Holy Father spoke in Westminster Hall in front of both Houses of Parliament and all former Prime Ministers, he addressed the role and history of Parliament in setting a righteous course and in showing moral leadership. Pope Benedict specifically mentioned the role of Parliament in the abolition of slavery.

Later, the Holy Father, sitting alongside the Archbishop of Canterbury, spoke about the role of faith in contemporary society and the importance of a fruitful dialogue between religion and reason, a theme he said 'as relevant in the time of Saint Thomas More as it is in our own day'. Pope Benedict's words spoke powerfully of the tradition of tolerance in the country. But most of all, it was the Pope's words on the international situation that left me with the greatest satisfaction. Why? Because so often people ask me what the Vatican does in foreign or international policy. Speaking in Westminster Hall, the Pope articulated the specific points of interaction between the United Kingdom and the Holy See. The Holy Father cited disarmament, including the Arms Trade Treaty and the Cluster Munitions Treaty, also mentioning the issue of Climate Change and the joint work to tackle its harmful effects. The Pope spoke powerfully of the need for development and he praised the Government's commitment to deliver 0.7 per cent of GDP to international development by 2013.

In all, the Pope delivered 15 sermons or speeches during his four-day visit. The Prime Minister, in bidding farewell to the Pope at Birmingham Airport, recalled the Pope's words and he spoke of the role of faith in our society. The Prime Minister also called for a deepening of the relationship between the United Kingdom and the Holy See.

The final memory that I am left with after the Papal Visit, was very much more personal. While at the Mass in Westminster Cathedral on 18 September, I kept recalling the last time I had seen a Papal Visit on these islands. It was 29 September 1979 when Pope John Paul II visited Drogheda. Many of the 300,000 people who attended that event had come from Northern Ireland as the Papal itinerary did not include Northern Ireland, because of the level of violence at that time. Though only nine at the time, I remember the Pope's words, 'On my knees I beg you to turn away from the paths of violence and return to the ways of peace.' It was a powerful message delivered by a Pope who had known more than his fair share of hardship.

During Pope Benedict's visit, I kept thinking about the events of 31 years ago and wondering whether I would see another Papal Visit to these islands in my lifetime. I thought of those who had brought me to see the Pope in Drogheda – all now deceased. The memories of 31 years earlier brought home to me what we were witnessing during these four days in September 2010. The Papal Visit of September 2010 has left me with life-long memories and who knows whether we will see another such visit again in our lifetimes. To have been able to accompany the Pope on this journey was an immense privilege and honour and a highlight of my personal and professional life.

An Address given by Cardinal Newman to the Catholic Truth Society

Cardinal Newman's Address to the Catholic Truth Society (of 1890)

In reply to an address presented to Cardinal Newman by the Catholic Truth Society, on the occasion of the CTS Conference at Birmingham in July, 1890, His Eminence said:

My dear friends,

I *wish, both in thought and language, as far as I can, to thank you, as I do very heartily.* I thank you for your affection - it is the affection of great souls. You are not common people. I could say a great deal, but I will only pray that God may sustain and put His confirmation upon what you do. I give you every good wish.

Your Society is one which makes us feel the sadness of the days through which we have passed, when the Church of Christ wanted those assistances of publication which Protestants possessed in such abundance. I envied both the matter and the intention of those publications. It is a cruel thing that our Faith has been debarred from the possibility of lively action, but it was no fault of Catholics. They have been so pressed and distracted from the formation of any policy, that the Church has had to depend on only a few heads and the management of a few. This has been the cause of the absence of interest and popularity in publications among Catholics. But now there is no reason why we should not have the power which has before this been in the hands of Protestants, whose zeal, however, I have always admired. But the reward is at hand for us, and we must thank God for giving to us such a hope. I may say of myself that I have had much sorrow that the hopes and the prospects of the Church have shown so little sign of brightening. There has been - there is now - a

A photograph of Father John Henry Newman taken in about 1865 by R W Thrupp of Birmingham

great opposition against the Church; but this time, and this day, are the beginnings of a revolution. I have had despondency; but the hour has come when we may make good use, and practical use, of the privileges which God has given us. We must thank God and ask for His best blessing and mercy. May He sustain you. God is not wanting if we are ready to work. I beg you to pardon and to forget the weakness of my words. I am content to pray for you and for your works.

God bless you.

PRAYER FOR THE CANONISATION OF BLESSED JOHN HENRY NEWMAN

G od our Father,

You granted to your servant Blessed John Henry Newman wonderful gifts of nature and of grace, that he should be a spiritual light in the darkness of this world, an eloquent herald of the Gospel, and a devoted servant of the one Church of Christ. With confidence in his heavenly intercession, we make the following petition: …

For his insight into the mysteries of the kingdom, his zealous defence of the teachings of the Church, and his priestly love for each of your children, we pray that he may soon be numbered among the Saints. We ask this through Christ our Lord.

Amen.

Nihil Obstat: The Reverand Father Pat McKinney
Imprimatur:
✠ Bernard Longley,
Archbishop of Birmingham.
30 March 2010

*The first class relic of Blessed John Henry Newman was placed in the reliquary outside
Saint Philip's Chapel in the Oratory Church, Edgbaston, for the Mass of Thanksgiving on
Monday 20 September 2010.*

Praise to the Holiest in the height
And in the depth be praise;
In all his words most wonderful,
Most sure in all his ways!

The Dream of Gerontius, by Blessed John Henry Newman

INTERNET RESOURCES

www.thepapalvisit.org.uk The Official Papal Visit website

www.newmanreader.org.uk The Newman Reader

www.indcatholicnews.com Independent Catholic News

www.vatican.va The official Vatican website

www.zenit.org Zenit International News Agency

www.newmanfriendsinternational.org International Centre of Newman Friends

www.newenglishorchestra.org The New English Orchestra